MW00962235

THE
SALT
FACTOR^2

THE SALT FACTOR²

Seasoning *Your* World *With* Jesus

SINO AGUEZE

XULON PRESS

Xulon Press
2301 Lucien Way #415
Maitland, FL 32751
407.339.4217
www.xulonpress.com

© 2020 by Sino Agueze

All rights reserved solely by the author. The author guarantees all contents are original and do not infringe upon the legal rights of any other person or work. No part of this book may be reproduced in any form without the permission of the author. The views expressed in this book are not necessarily those of the publisher.

Unless otherwise indicated, Scripture quotations taken from the King James Version (KJV) – *public domain.*

Scripture quotations taken from the New King James Version (NKJV). Copyright © 1982 by Thomas Nelson, Inc. Used by permission. All rights reserved.

Scripture quotations taken from The Message (MSG). Copyright © 1993, 1994, 1995, 1996, 2000, 2001, 2002. Used by permission of NavPress Publishing Group. Used by permission. All rights reserved.

Scripture quotations taken from the Holy Bible, New Living Translation (NLT). Copyright ©1996, 2004, 2007 by Tyndale House Foundation. Used by permission of Tyndale House Publishers, Inc.

Scripture taken from The Passion Translation (TPT). Copyright © 2017 by Passion & Fire Ministries, Inc. Used by permission. All rights reserved. thePassionTranslation.com

Scripture quotations taken from the Amplified Bible (AMP). Copyright © 1954, 1958, 1962, 1964, 1965, 1987 by The Lockman Foundation. Used by permission. All rights reserved.

Scripture quotations taken from The **Voice** Bible (VB) Copyright © 2012 Thomas Nelson, Inc. The Voice™ translation © 2012 Ecclesia Bible Society All rights reserved.

(also GW) Scripture quotations taken from the Gods Word Translation copyright ©1995 by Baker Publishing Group.

(also the GNB) Scripture quotations taken from the Good News Translation (GNT). Copyright © 1992 American Bible Society. Used by permission. All rights reserved.

Scripture quotations taken from the Weymouth New Testament (WNT) – *public domain.*

Scripture quotations taken from the Holy Bible, New International Version (NIV). Copyright © 1973, 1978, 1984, 2011 by Biblica, Inc.™. Used by permission. All rights reserved.

Paperback ISBN-13: 978-1-6312-9905-6
Hard Cover ISBN-13: 978-1-6322-1016-6
Ebook ISBN-13: 978-1-6312-9906-3

CONTENTS:

DEDICATION

This book is dedicated to all yearning not only to live a life of significance, but also, to those who want to wholeheartedly live for the Lord Jesus Christ. It is dedicated to those who choose to live ordinarily in an extraordinary way. It is for those who have decided that all about them must be all about Him. It is dedicated to everyone who has refused to live by the status-quo, breaking out of all forms of limitations and ceilings stifling the gifts within designed for the blessing of humanity. It is for those who walk in the knowledge that they've been born for this season and for a people as saviors born in Zion.

INTRODUCTION

This book is all about how the Church, the body of Christ, the people of God, by necessity, need to redefine and reposition themselves to find importance, significance and above all, relevance in today's culture. We know that the central message of the gospel of our Lord Jesus Christ doesn't and shouldn't change, but how to make it both relevant and powerful in a post-modern culture would to a large extent determine the impact the gospel would have on the people of the 21st century and beyond. To help achieve this goal, we must take another look at our understanding of the Great Commission, which is the Lord's most important corporate assignment and mission statement for all the body of Christ. This book would endeavor to define what the Great Commission is with clarity and precision. How would we accomplish the mandate of the Great Commission if we have an improper or an unbalanced view of the Great Commission? What if we've ignorantly or erroneously held onto a long-old-aged view that has rendered the Church ineffective in reaching the lost in today's culture. Like everything else, when we've lost our way, we go back to the beginning to find the ancient landmarks to help us get back on track. I am totally convinced that a better, fuller and truer under-standing of the Great Commission would produce in and for us a more powerful and transformative way not only to make the gospel of our Lord Jesus Christ relevant in today's culture, but also, create a new and complete paradigm shift in the way we ought to do Church in this generation.

CHAPTER 1

THE GREAT COMMISSION DEFINED
"OUR KINGDOM CORPORATE ASSIGNMENT"

There's a need to fully, but accurately define the Great Commission so that its full meaning is grasped, and nothing is left to presumptions or illusions. By targeting its true meaning, we capture the heart of God and narrow our focus within those boundaries. Here, our obedience becomes comprehensibly simple and applicably forceful. We've endeavored to offer four definitions. All four definitions given on the Great Commission are coherent to each other, and also singularly unique in their depth, meaning and usage. The student must pay close attention to how each definition is a part of the whole and is incomplete, standing by itself. They are like the "four faces" in Ezekiel's Chariot revealing the completeness of the Christ and are all needed to help grasp the full meaning of the Great Commission.

SOME FACTS ABOUT THE GREAT COMMISSION

- First, the Great Commission is a commandment, but it is no ordinary commandment.
- Second, the Great Commission is God's last will and testament given to each individual member of the Church, His bride. It is the most important corporate commandment charged to the body of Christ. It is a collective mandate requiring a collective cooperation.
- Third, all of the work of Christ, including the work of his cross and the work of the resurrection culminate into the commandment to disciple the nations of the earth.
- Fourth, all the work and the success of the New Testament Church must be measured in line with the commandment to disciple the nations of the earth. The Great Commission becomes the yardstick for measuring all true progress in the kingdom of God.

THE FOUR DEFINITIONS OF THE GREAT COMMISSION

DEFINITION 1

The Great Commission is the commandment to disciple the nations of the earth.

Go therefore and make disciples of all the nations, baptizing them in the name of the Father and of the Son and of the Holy Spirit,
Matthew 28:19 NKJV

The Great Commission is all about the discipleship of nations, and not simply the discipleship of people. The discipleship of nations produces far more results in leading many lost souls to Jesus Christ than all the evangelistic campaigns combined. Many discipleship experts have limited this Scripture to the disciplining of converts, and as a consequence, have provided an improper view of this passage robbing us of its fuller and more comprehensive meaning. Nations are built upon seven structures and by transforming or discipling these seven structures, you disciple the nation. The focus here in fulfilling the Great Commission, therefore, must become the discipleship of the seven structures upon which a nation is built.

Therefore, the Great Commission is God's call upon the Church to disciple the nations of the earth. We're to baptize the nations of the earth into a three-fold baptism of the nature and character of the Father, Son and Holy Spirit.

DEFINITION 2
The Great Commission is about establishing God's reign in all strata of society.

You watched while a stone was cut out without hands, which struck the image on its feet of iron and clay, and broke them in pieces. Then the iron, the clay, the bronze, the silver, and the gold were crushed together, and became like chaff from the summer threshing floors; the wind carried them away so that no trace of them was found. And the stone that struck the image became a great mountain and filled the whole earth.

Daniel 2:34-35 NKJV

Daniel's interpretation of the King's dream reveals that the kingdoms of this world would come to an end, and that the kingdom of God would become like a great mountain filling the whole earth. God's reign in the earth was never designed to be instantaneous but progressive. It's happening in the here and now. God plans to set up His kingdom during the reign of the kings of the earth.

And in the days of these kings the God of heaven will set up a kingdom which shall never be destroyed; and the kingdom shall not be left to other people; it shall break in pieces and consume all these kingdoms, and it shall stand forever. Inasmuch as you saw that the stone

was cut out of the mountain without hands, and that it broke in pieces the iron, the bronze, the clay, the silver, and the gold—the great God has made known to the king what will come to pass after this. The dream is certain, and its interpretation is sure."

Daniel 2:44-45 NKJV

Jesus spoke a parable about this progressive take-over of the kingdoms of the earth, and He spoke it for two reasons: because they thought that he was near Jerusalem and that the kingdom of God would immediately appear.

And Jesus said to him, "Today salvation has come to this house, because he also is a son of Abraham; for the Son of Man has come to seek and to save that which was lost." Now as they heard these things, He spoke another parable, because He was near Jerusalem and because they thought the kingdom of God would appear immediately. Therefore He said: "A certain nobleman went into a far country to receive for himself a kingdom and to return. So he called ten of his servants, delivered to them ten minas, and said to them, 'Do

business till I come.' But his citizens hated him, and sent a delegation after him, saying, 'We will not have this man to reign over us.'

Luke 19:9-14 NKJV

Filling the earth with God's glory would always remain an important aspect of God's plan (Numbers 14:21) — a plan that was inaugurated from the beginning of time (Genesis 1:26). Scripturally, the kingdoms of this world must become the kingdom of our God and of His Christ (Revelation 11:15); not after the rapture or during the millennium, but right now on earth (Daniel 2:44-45; Isaiah 9:7; Luke 19:10-27). Every strata and sphere of society must be saturated and dominated with the rule of God until it becomes His rightful domain – a microcosm of the kingdom of God.

DEFINITION 3
The Great Commission is the art of displacing and replacing value systems.

Value systems make or break a nation. Satan's primary method of controlling the nations of the world comes through entrenching the seven spheres of society with its deadly and demonic value systems. It's easy to tell who's in control of a nation or a sphere of a nation by examining the predominate value system at work.

Whereas you saw the feet and toes, partly of potter's clay and partly of iron, the kingdom shall be divided; yet the strength of the iron shall be in it, just as you saw the iron mixed with ceramic clay. And as the toes of the feet were partly of iron and partly of clay, so the kingdom shall be partly strong and partly fragile. As you saw iron mixed with ceramic clay, they will mingle with the seed of men; but they will not adhere to one another, just as iron does not mix with clay.

Daniel 2:41-43 NKJV

Daniel again shows us that the devil is chiefly responsible for weakening the nations of the earth — Isaiah 14:12. In his interpretation of the king's dream, he refers the clay in the image as the potter's clay. Who's the potter pottering the clay? The answer is the devil. And how does he weaken the nations? He doesn't primarily through injecting his value systems into the very fiber of a nation until it mutates into a nation's DNA. The Scriptures show us that the women would mingle themselves with the seed of men, but that they would not cleave one to another. In other words, God's value system of the male and female marriage institution would be subverted and perverted by the devil. The whole family structure would come under the full siege of the devil. Satan will introduce doctrines of demons and recreate the entire culture of a nation.

America as a nation not too long ago was heading into hell in a handbasket when the neutral-gender ideology was being boldly and proudly championed by a beloved president. Deadly pro-choice policies thrived under this same presidency. America had so fallen from the norm that policies on the shared use of public restrooms by both male and females were making headline news on a daily basis; because, as they said, we shouldn't discriminate between the sexes. America was on the verge of completely losing all moral fiber and compass. Many so-called Christians were so blinded by their love for the president that they came up with the excuse that we cannot legislate righteousness. However, the devil didn't mind legislating unrighteousness as these same believers lived passively comatose as if under a spell. There wasn't a single voice raised or a cry heard against this immoral pandemic eating away at the life source of a nation. And as goes America, so goes the rest of the world. Satan had built his citadel at Washington. Christianity was at 4% among teens at this time, and churches were struggling to grow. The entire atmosphere in the nation had become so demonic that anyone could cut the darkness present with a machete. For the first time, the DNC voted God out of the nation. Prayer and Bible studies at public schools were declared unconstitutional. Christians were threatened with lawsuits and were forbidden to speak against sin. We were labeled with all sorts of names ranging from being homophobic to being out-dated and not in touch with reality. Abominable life-styles were welcomed and celebrated on church pulpits with pride. And in-spite of this moral decay, no one felt the mourning of the church.

We know that we are God's children and that the whole world lies under the misery and influence of the Evil One.
1 John 5:19 TPT

We know [for a fact] that we are of God, and the whole world [around us] lies in the power of the evil one [opposing God and His precepts].
1 John 5:19 AMP

An entire nation can come under the devil's spell. An entire people can be made drunk with the wine of her fornication. Demonic ideologies can sway over a nation transforming it into the devil's paradise. The Great Commission was given to the church to displace the value systems of this world and replace them with the value systems of the kingdom of God. Value systems serve as primers. They prime a nation for a move of God or for a move of Satan. They prime a nation where righteousness reigns or where the law of sin and death reigns. They make a society conducive for the propagation of the gospel of Jesus Christ or become a stumbling block for the gospel as is presently the case with Japan and North Korea and many other nations.

DEFINITION 4

The Great Commission is the transformation of both the soul of the man and his environment.

So the Lord God took the man [He had made] and settled him in the Garden of Eden to cultivate and keep it.
Genesis 2:15 AMP

The Great Commission is not limited to the transformation of the soul of man, It also extends to the transformation or discipleship of the man's environment. Think about impoverished places were all types of vices exist. You visit such a place bearing the glad tidings of the gospel. A resident responds favorably to the message and becomes a born-again Christian. However, this new babe in Christ goes back to living in the same impoverished environment surrounded with the worst vices on the planet day and night. In such a surrounding with all of its inhibiting vices, how much of a good witness would this new believer in Christ become for his Lord and Savior, Jesus Christ? I am not saying it is impossible to thrive as a disciple of Jesus Christ by reason of a powerful and dramatic transformation by the saving grace of the Holy Spirit upon the human heart; but the fervent lifestyle of this newborn babe is highly unlikely to become sustainable over a long period of time. We will have to assume that this precious soul growing up in such a surrounding has to some degree been previously scared and deeply wounded in the soul. He will have to constantly struggle with his own inner vices as well as his outer vices impeding his spiritual growth. He may be saved, but ineffective as a witness or disciple. It's like leaving a former alcoholic with alcoholics and alcohol day and night. Such an environment is not an empowering one but an enabling one.

God went through a six-day creation of an uninhabitable and chaotic earth to create a suitable environment for man so that he can grow and thrive as a manager over God's planet. This environment, a microcosm of the kingdom of heaven, was to become the home and the office of the human species. This heaven on earth environment was intentionally designed and built by God to help bring out the best in man as God's vice regent in the earth.

Therefore, the Great Commission not only saves a man, but also saves or redeems his environment. The Great Commission is transformational by nature. It transforms the man and the man's landscape. It disciples the heart and soul of a man, and the very culture of the land. It changes everything it touches. It transforms the political, social, educational and economic fiber of a nation. Soul winning efforts or evangelistic campaigns only transform the heart of a man, but does not by itself transform man's surroundings. The Great Commission was given to achieve both.

WHY THE GREAT COMMISSION?

Why did Jesus give us the commandment on the Great Commission or the divine corporate assignment? In other words, what were His specific reasons for asking us or rather commanding us to make the discipleship of nations the church's priority?

He gave us the commandment to win the world to Himself. God not only desires that entire nations be saved (Revelation 21:24), but that the whole world would be saved. He gave us the Great Commission for that one goal. But first, we must realize that the entire cosmos is under the complete influence of the wicked one.

> **We know that we are God's children and that the whole world lies under the misery and influence of the Evil One.**
> **1 John 5:19 TPT**

HOW DOES THE WORLD COME UNDER THE INFLUENCE OF SATAN?

The book of revelation and the book of Daniel explains how nations come under the spell of the evil one. It is important that we understand this because it is a major reason why Jesus gave us this commandment to disciple the nations of the earth.

> **And there came one of the seven angels which had the seven vials, and talked with me, saying unto me, Come hither; I will shew unto thee the judgment of the great whore that sitteth upon many waters: With whom the kings of the earth have committed fornication, and the inhabitants of the earth have been made drunk with the wine of her fornication.**
>
> **Revelation 17:1-2 KJV**

This whore, the spirit of Babylon, sits as queen upon many waters. This means that she sits in a place of dominion, as one in-charge. And what are these many waters that she's sitting upon?

> **And he saith unto me, The waters which thou sawest, where the whore sitteth, are peoples, and multitudes, and nations, and tongues.**
>
> **Revelation 17:15 KJV**

This spirit is sitting upon peoples, multitudes, nations and tongues. Can a spirit exercise such authority of the nations of the earth? The answer is an absolute yes. This spirit of Babylon first commits fornication with the kings of the earth, and then with the earth's inhabitants. She goes after the people in power — the people with the power to turn the tide of nations. She goes after the leadership: political, religious, economic, social, educational; including state actors in all fields of life. She goes after anyone who has the power to influence people, so that, through their influence, she can take an entire people or nation hostage to her will. They use the media houses a lot as well as the entertainment industry since they weigh a heavy amount of influence on the world. To get the people, the inhabitants, she must go after their kings. This is how the inhabitants come under the wine of her fornication.

The book of Daniel reveals the double kingdom. Lurking behind the political powers of the earth are mighty spiritual forces shaping the culture and the destiny of nations.

Then said he unto me, Fear not, Daniel: for from the first day that thou didst set thine heart to understand, and to chasten thyself before thy God, thy words were heard, and I am come for thy words. But the prince of the kingdom of Persia withstood me one and twenty days: but, lo, Michael, one

**of the chief princes, came to help me;
and I remained there with the kings
of Persia.**

Daniel 10:12-13 KJV

The angel told Daniel that the prince of the kingdom of Persia, and the kings of Persia withstood him for twenty-one days. Did you notice how emphatic the archangel of God, Gabriel, describes their names and offices? The spiritual kings of Persia serve under the crown prince of the kingdom of Persia. Every government in every nation on earth has a double kingdom. One in the natural, and the other one in the spiritual. The spiritual kingdom, if permitted, always influences the natural kingdom. These demonic spirits introduce ideologies, philosophies, policies etc. to sway an entire nation to Satan's will. Their main goal is to displace the value systems of the kingdom of God, and replace them with values forged in hell.

**Here is the mind possessing wisdom:
The seven heads signify the seven
mountains where the woman is seated.
They also stand for seven kings.**

Revelation 17:9 VOICE

SOME FACTS ABOUT THE WHORE SITTING UPON SEVEN MOUNTAINS

- The world is made up of continents, and continents, nations.
- Every nation or society is built upon seven fundamental structures.

The seven (7) structures are as follows:
- Government/Politics
- Business/Economy
- Education
- Mass Media
- Arts, Sports and Entertainment
- Religion
- Family

Each of these structures is built on a value system.
- Every value system is sourced in either God or Satan.
- The predominant value system reveals who is in control.
- Nations are controlled by the beliefs of its value systems.
- To transform a nation or society, its value system must be transformed.

It is of paramount importance that Satan corrupt all seven structures. He subverts and perverts them. Like a container, he fills them up with value systems from hades. He is fully aware that every child born into this world or into this Canaanite culture must pass through one or more of these structures, pillars or tunnels. The goal is to shape the people's mindset, belief system and culture with the established demonic value systems so that they grow up without the consciousness of God. He primes nations to disbelieve the gospel of the Lord Jesus Christ. He longs to build a society of people to become antagonistic to the gospel of Jesus, so that, they would not be saved, and join him in the lake of fire. By controlling the mindsets and character-culture of an entire people, he controls their destiny. He achieves this through the structures that must mold mankind – through the seven institutions that men must pass through in this life. Therefore, by examining your nation's structures and the value-systems in each structure, you can easily tell who is in control of your nation. Because of this very reason, Jesus gave us the commandment to disciple the nations of the earth, and we call this the commandment of the Great Commission.

THE NO.1 GOAL OF EVERY LOCAL CHURCH AND ITS PASTOR

A) Knowing How to Measure True Kingdom Success
How do we measure true kingdom success? How are we to determine that we are on track with the

commandment to disciple the nations of the earth? The three following fundamental points must be comprehended if we are to become relevant to God as a church, and they are:

- We would need to thoroughly understand what God defines as success
- Our success must be measured in line with the Great Commission.
- It is measured primarily by the wealth of God's values at work in a nation.

Success in today's churches and other para-ministries are completely different from what God would regard as success. Many would simply not qualify as a successful church in the eyes of God, although, they may qualify as one in the eyes of men. The Great Commission mandate is God's yardstick for measuring success in the Kingdom. Do not forget God's primary and original purpose for creating man, which was, and still is, to establish God's reign in all the earth. See: Numbers 14:21; Isaiah 9:7, Daniel 2:44-45 and Rev. 11:15. The real question now is, "how much of God's value system can be seen in each of the structures on which your nation is built? How much of it can be seen in the family structure or the educational structure or the business structure? It is, therefore, no longer measured by simply the share size of your congregation or the size of your offerings or the influence of your T.V.

programs or how big of a name you have in the community, but by the actual work and the success of that work in the marketplace.

B). Raising Savior-Kings

> **And saviours shall come up on mount Zion to judge the mount of Esau; and the kingdom shall be the Lord's.**
> **Obadiah 1:21 KJV**

Zion, the church, is a breeding ground for raising saviors. And these saviors live to judge the mount of Esau, so that, the kingdom can become the Lord's.

Jesus, too, was born a Savior-King — Luke 2:11. We shall talk more about this in chapter two. The primary goal of every single pastor and every local church is to raise societal saviors also known as the "Sons of the Kingdom" and/or "Savior-Kings." The harvest of the end time solely depends on the quality of "sons" raised. This is a fundamental difference between "Soul-Winning" and the "Great Commission." The former deals with producing babes, while the latter deals with raising sons. One son is better than ten thousand babes – (2 Samuel 18:3). The truth is, there are very few "Sons" in the kingdom today. This is why over 90% of the world's population is yet to be saved and why 96% of its structures are yet to become filled with the value-systems of God. Is this success? The time to

19

think differently is now; but unfortunately, many pastors have a contained and confined local mindset. The question for the Pastor and his Church is, "are you raising "sons," and do you know how to do it? Don't forget however that it takes a father to raise a son.

THE SEVEN (7) CHARATERISTICS OF A SOCIETAL SAVIOR

- His greatest call is to be like Christ in practice
- He must take his place as a sent one
- His calling is relational to one or more of the seven structures of society
- He must master the sphere he has been called to dominate
- He must function in the 4-Fold ministry traits of the Holy Spirit
- His calling is to solve a societal ill
- It takes kingdom structures and systems to sustain all kingdom efforts

Chapter 2

SALT IN A SALTSHAKER
"SAVIORS IN ZION"

We all use saltshakers at home and at restaurants. We need it to season or flavor our meals. The saltshaker preserves the salt within the salt container. But the salt in the shaker is primarily meant to be poured out of its shaker or container. In a similar way, the church, God's people, were never meant to stay imprisoned within the four walls of the church. This is not where her true power lies. Her true power is in having her poured out into the world around her. For centuries, Pastors have acted like wardens, and they've kept their members imprisoned. We've defined church as having Sunday and midweek services. People tend to live their own lives Monday through Saturday, and then show up for an hour or two to have church on a Sunday. Many go home after the Sunday service with the feeling that they've done the Christian "thing." The rest of the Sunday day is given to family time, meals and watching sports. This scenario plays out pretty much the same way week after week, and somehow, over the years, has become accepted as the norm in so many quarters. If this is what the church is, then, it would be impossible to reach the world for Jesus even with a thousand lifetimes over. We've done a good job preserving the saints within the four walls, but a very poor job in releasing her into her God assigned destiny. We've failed to release her to walk into her divine design, and to live out the reason for her very existence. Like salt within the saltshaker, she's lost sight of her true power. The power of salt happens when, and only when it's poured out of its container. The power of the church happens when the people are released to do and live ministry outside the four walls.

REDEFINING CHURCH FOR TODAY

Church shouldn't be defined by one hundred percent of the people attending service for two hours on Sunday morning, while they live their own lives from Monday through Saturday. That's two hours for God, and a hundred and sixty-six hours for everything else under the sun per week. How can we win the world to Christ living this way? Let's flip this: what if one percent of the people do the work of the ministry Monday through Saturday for a hundred and sixty-six hours per week actively involved in the marketplace? What if the body of Jesus Christ lived out the kingdom mandate of the Great Commission Monday through Saturday in the marketplace? Would this way of doing ministry produce a far greater impact for the kingdom of God? Now people, that's the church. On Sunday mornings, we get trained, discipled and equipped to do the work of the ministry. On Sunday mornings, we celebrate the spoils of war. However, Mondays through Saturdays, we live with the consciousness of a soul winner out there in the marketplace. What a paradigm shift that would be — a totally different way of doing church.

> **The mighty God, even the LORD, hath spoken, and called the earth from the rising of the sun unto the going down thereof. Out of Zion, the perfection of beauty, God hath shined.**
>
> **Psalms 50:1-2 KJV**

SOME ERRONEOUS CONCEPTS OF WHAT A CHURCH IS

- Some think the church exists simply to increase membership
- Some think the church exists to promote a specific denomination
- Some view the church as a charitable organization
- Some think the church is for weak people
- Some think it is a place for spiritual experiences or breakthroughs
- Some view it is a place where great messages are taught

- Some view it as a place of fellowship or a support system
- Some view it as something they are "supposed" to do as a Christian
- Some think it is a place to gain an identity or self-worth

REDEFINING DISCIPLESHIP

Have you ever noticed that Jesus never discipled a single soul in a classroom setting? That was not His chosen method or strategy. The Bible tells us how He did it.

> **And he ordained twelve, that they should be with him, and that he might send them forth to preach.**
>
> **Mark 3:14 KJV**

> **Wherefore of these men which have companied with us all the time that the Lord Jesus went in and out among us, Beginning from the baptism of John, unto that same day that he was taken up from us, must one be ordained to be a witness with us of his resurrection.**
>
> **Acts 1:21-22 KJV**

His disciples lived with Him, walked with Him, and followed Him for three and a half years, beginning at the baptism of John until He was taken up into glory. Jesus discipled them while on the go out there in the streets, villages and city lanes. They were witnesses of His life and ministry. They all did life together outside the four walls where real ministry happened. They were firsthand witnesses of His life, His works, His miracles, and His interactions with people. He discipled them by modeling His life in an experiential setting. Jesus knew the training was real with real people who had real problems in real life situations. Classroom training is mostly all theory with little to no action. Police officers sitting at the desk know that there's no action there; it's all in the field. The church of today has become an amoeba church. An amoeba is a one celled organism that lives for itself; it does not have the capacity to reproduce. They are shapeless and formless, and this explains why today's church has been experiencing little to no real transformational power.

I believe wholeheartedly that Jesus, the Lord of the church, designed His body to grow spiritually while on the go. A major part of our growth in Christ takes place while we're on the job doing the father's business. All that stuff we call ministry: ushering, greeting, singing etc. is simply keeping house. But real ministry happens on the outside. I equally believe that this is why there are little to no miraculous manifestations of the Spirit. Jesus may have performed one or two miracles in the synagogue, but all the other miracles took place while He was on the go.

> **And he said unto them, Go ye into all the world, and preach the gospel to every creature. And they went forth, and preached every where, the Lord working with them, and confirming the word with signs following. Amen.**
>
> **Mark 16:15, 20 KJV**

The Lord worked with them as they went, and not as they stayed, confirming their words with signs following. Only when we take on the biblical model for growth in the kingdom shall all the apostolic gifts be restored to the church.

Chapter 3

HOW SALT WORKS IN A SOUP
"KINGDOM PRINCIPLES FOR TRANSFORMING WORLD SYSTEMS"

And he said, Bring me a new cruse, and put salt therein. And they brought it to him. And he went forth unto the spring of the waters, and cast the salt in there, and said, Thus saith the LORD, I have healed these waters; there shall not be from thence any more death or barren land.

2 Kings 2:20-21 KJV

The Lord healed and transformed the waters in the above Scriptures by using salt, which was poured out into the spring of a dead and barren sea. As believers in Christ Jesus, we've become the salt of the earth, and it is now a part of our nature to bring healing and transformation to the world around us. Jesus said, "have salt in yourselves — Mark 9:50. As salt out of its shaker, we as believers need to be poured out into the waters of this world. Only as we are poured out can we preserve, restore and bring life to the people of this world through Jesus Christ. The dead waters represent a world without Jesus — it's a lost world; a dead world.

THE SEVEN PRINCIPLES ON HOW TO CHANGE A COMMUNITY

PRINCIPLE ONE:
GET THE SALT OUT OF THE SALTSHAKER
(REAL MINISTRY IS MINISTRY OUTSIDE THE FOUR WALLS OF THE CHURCH)

Imagine what would happen once the body of Christ lays a hold of this paradigm shift. The shift where a hundred percent of the church is actively engaged in the business of the Great Commission all week long. A shift where our understanding of doing church is no longer based on our two hours of Sunday mornings services; rather, it is based on living the gospel the other one hundred and sixty-six hours of the week. The business of fully engaging people in the marketplace becomes our redefinition of doing church and being the church.

PHAROAH LET MY PEOPLE GO

Let's try and settle this fact once and for all: God's people belong to God. The church is His bride, He bought her with His own blood, and no pastor should publicly or privately claim a church as his personal belonging. Overseeing or overprotecting the church should never be used as an excuse to lord over a people as if they personally belonged to you. The Lord Jesus, and only the Lord Jesus, should have the full and rightful claim over His own bride. Pastors, release the people to fulfill God's vision over their lives. Every child of God came into this world with a God vision. A big part of our responsibilities as pastors and leaders who have been entrusted with overseeing the sheep of His pasture is to help interpret the dreams and visions that God has placed upon their lives. In other words, help them discover the one thing they were born to do with their lives. Help them make that vision a kingdom vision, and help equip them to fulfill that calling. Disciple them to become greater than yourself. Help them do the greater works than you did. Let the people go! You grow a church by sending people out, and not by hoarding them or imprisoning them. Raise the people up with a real mission minded mentality. Simply put: release God's people into ministry. The true power of the church doesn't lie within her four walls, the same way that the true power of salt doesn't lie within the saltshaker. A particular church may be experiencing the best revival in town or even a strong move of God, but if all that power remains within the four walls, it would eventually die. On the day of Pentecost, the 120 disciples experienced an outpouring of the Holy Spirit unlike anything that has ever been seen before; and yet, they came out of that upper room into the streets the same day of the outpouring where three thousand lost souls got saved. God's power and anointing makes us witnesses of Jesus, and not church members. His fire baptism upon our lives should thrusts us all out into the harvest field. The oil of the prophet's widow flows only when it is poured out to fill every available empty vessel. Yes, the oil is primarily a missional anointing. Pastors, send the people out to go fulfill the commandment of the Great Commission. Get the salt out of its saltshaker. Paul and Barnabas were teachers and prophets bound to the four walls of the church, until the Holy Spirit said, "separate me Barnabas and Saul unto the work to which I have called them" — Acts 13:2. Most of the church are hoarding churches, and not sending churches. Imagine raising an entire army of God's people with a missional kingdom mentality.

DO NOT FORGET YOUR JERUSALEM

> **But ye shall receive power, after that
> the Holy Ghost is come upon you: and
> ye shall be witnesses unto me both in
> Jerusalem, and in all Judaea, and in**

Samaria, and unto the uttermost part of the earth.

Acts 1:8 KJV

Missions should not be thought of only in terms of traveling abroad or to a foreign country. We need to have a strong "Jerusalem Missions Mindset." That's missions at the home front too. Our neighborhoods, villages, communities, towns and cities need the impact of the gospel as much as anywhere else. True evangelism is when the church, God's people, actively engage people in the marketplace on a daily basis as a daily lifestyle that's in the malls, coffee houses, grocery stores, workplaces, or anywhere people are. Am talking about a one-on-one and a face-to-face engagement with people in a proactive way. And that shouldn't be difficult if it comes across naturally since most people are open to talking anyway. If we all lived consumed with a soul winner's mindset on a daily basis, we would find ourselves making tremendous impact for the gospel of the Lord Jesus Christ in leading so many souls to Christ. Would a day like this ever come upon us? I pray so. Thrusting people out into the mission field can only happen by the mighty work of the Holy Spirit. And that work of the Spirit only happens when we pray — Matthew 9:37-38.

Unfortunately, we've defined ministry as singing, ushering, greeting, and all the other internal host of activities that go on to keep the church operational.

Although all of that is some type of "serving the body," it does not encompass the definition of true ministry. True ministry involves the public boldness of sharing one's faith — the exercise of which helps to truly mature us in our growth in Christ in a way that nothing else can. In so many contemporary churches where all the people have to do is invite the lost to church, and then leave the responsibility of saving the lost solely to the pastor may first appear to be effective, but it is robbing the members from the experience of knowing how to truly seek and save the lost in a way that produces a much more deeper and significant work of the Holy Spirit in their own lives. We've all being commissioned to do the work of an evangelist, and to carry out the mandate of the Great Commission. All believers should be discipled in the art of leading the lost to Christ as naturally as living one's daily life on a daily basis.

PRINCIPLE TWO
THE SALT MUST ENTER INTO THE SOUP
(STRATEGICALLY REPOSITION GOD'S PEOPLE INTO THEIR PROMISED LAND)

The church must become intentionally involved in the systems of this world, and not be afraid or timid of fully engaging the culture and its influence. God wants His church actively involved in today's culture, not isolated from it. Christians are called to be big players in the marketplace, and not to simply stand passively on the sidelines — Matt 11:16-17. In order to change a system, believers must first be taught and trained on how to penetrate the system to transform it from within without conforming to it. This only happens by understanding a specific system and how it works. God used Moses, who grew up in an Egyptian system to deliver a people bound by its system. God's supernatural abilities came on Moses' knowledge of the natural to help deliver the people out of a system. Jesus used disciples who grew up in a Jewish system to birth the kingdom system within the same religious system. God delivered the Apostle Paul from a people and a system and sent him back to it to transform it from the inside out — Acts 26:13-16. The church should not remain primitive in her thinking in this specific regard. She is in the world for a reason: to help transform it, and to infuse into it the value systems of the kingdom of God. Therefore, Pastors and other leaders would need to raise people up with the intent to strategically plant them into the seven spheres of society. Even God knew that to change the world and its values, He Himself had to become a part of it by taking on the nature of a man — Hebrews 2:14; Philippians 2:5-9.

Ye are the light of the world. A city that is set on a hill cannot be hid. Neither do men light a candle, and put it under a bushel, but on a candlestick; and it giveth light unto all that are in the house. Let

your light so shine before men, that they may see your good works, and glorify your Father which is in heaven.

Matthew 5:14-16 KJV

It's all about how the candlestick is placed in the room, isn't it? It has to be placed in the best spot where the room can receive the greatest illumination possible. That's doing things strategically. In the same way, God's people need to be discipled to enter into the seven pillars of a society and infuse it with the value systems of the kingdom of God.

DANIEL AND HIS COMPANIONS WERE TEN TIMES BETTER THAN THE BEST

Children in whom was no blemish, but well favoured, and skillful in all wisdom, and cunning in knowledge, and understanding science, and such as had ability in them to stand in the king's palace, and whom they might teach the learning and the tongue of the Chaldeans. And in all matters of wisdom and understanding, that the king enquired of them, he found them ten times better than all the magicians and astrologers that were in all his realm.

Daniel 1:4, 20 KJV

King Nebuchadnezzar had commanded that certain of the children of Israel be brought down to Babylon, and to learn the literature and sciences of the land. They were given three years to accomplish this task. And at the end of their training, the king himself decided to carry out the final exam, and found all four of them ten times better than the best in every single subject of knowledge. We, the believers in Christ Jesus should be the best in all endeavors of life. We should be ten times better in the natural and the supernatural things of life. We should be so far ahead of the curve, that it would take the rest of the world decades or centuries to catch up to us. This was how King Solomon ruled the world during his time via the operation of the unmatched wisdom of God. The entire world sought him out.

HOW DO WE GET GOD'S PEOPLE INTO THESE SYSTEMS?

Each person's calling is where their pain and their passion intersect. There's something in the world that troubles you more than most, and you often feel deeply compelled to change it or do something significant about it. That's a strong indication of your calling. Specific problems tend to gravitate toward you because God has placed in you the solution to solve that problem. Since our relevance in God's kingdom is connected to fulfilling the Great Commission, our calling or pain and passion must address one or more of these seven structures. Within these seven main structures are sub-structures. Take for instance, within the family structure, you'll find the following sub-structures:

- **Great Grand Parents**
- **Grand Parents**
- **Parents**
- **Married Seniors**
- **Older Married Couples**
- **Younger Married Couples**
- **Older Widows**
- **Younger Widows**
- **Older Divorcees**
- **Younger Divorcees**
- **Young Adults**
- **Adolescents**
- **Teens**
- **Pre-Teens**
- **Children**
- **Infants**

Just within the family structure, we find about sixteen substructures. God's people who are being discipled through the local church would have to be taught to identify with a specific structure and/or substructure. Once that identification happens, then, they'll have to learn everything there's to learn about it with the goal of infusing into it the value systems of the kingdom of God. In God's kingdom, therefore, there are political pastors, business pastors, educational pastors, mass media pastors, arts, sports and entertainment pastors, religious pastors and family pastors. Do not allow the traditional definition of a pastor to throw you off. We're focusing on its functionality rather. A pastor or shepherd is one who tends, cares, feeds and guides the sheep. Each of us have been called to shepherd our own promised lands or our own specific spheres of influence. No one can change a system from the outside. It happens from the inside out. Eggs must break from the inside out to produce life. It is impossible to produce life from the outside in. Our own Savior exemplified this principle when He became the eternal "word" made human, and lived among the human race for thirty years, growing up in the culture of the day, and speaking the language of the day ever before He fully commenced His ministry. All of His parables clearly revealed that He used the language of the people to help communicate His message. He fully identified with the system of His day but not in a comprising way.

PRINCIPLE THREE
THE SALT LOSES ITS OUTWARD CRYSTALLINE SHELL
(IT'S ALL ABOUT IMPACT AND NOT ABOUT OUR RELIGIOUS CLICHES)

Whenever we use salt to season our meals or flavor something we've got cooking on a stove or cooker, the crystalline shell dissolves in the pot. The salt in a cooking pot loses its white or pink crystalline color upon saturation. This mutation is an example of a very powerful principle in the transformation of whole communities. Salt can be easily identified by its crystalline shell, but it is bought and used only because of its transformational properties. In other words, it is known and used for its impact purposes; that is, its ability to flavor food.

Let your light so shine before men, that they may see your good works, and glorify your Father which is in heaven.
Matthew 5:16 KJV

The gospel of the Great Commission includes works — convincing works that cause people to glorify our Father who is in heaven. I call it the gospel of undeniable results. One language the world cannot refute is the language of results. Who in their right mind can deny the results or proofs staring at them smack in the middle of their faces? Salt is all about its power to flavor food. No one cares much about its looks.

WE CAN'T WIN THE WORLD OVER WITH OUR DENOMINATIONAL LABELS OR DOCTRINES.

Our denominational labels, which didn't exist in the church in "Acts," has done nothing to lead the lost to

Jesus. These labels are often with good intentions, as a means of protecting the rights and beliefs of a particular Christian group. However, we've spent way too much time fighting on our own particular and peculiar doctrinal correctness. Doctrine is vitally important, but the point is, the world doesn't care about them. The central message preached by the Apostles and disciples of Jesus all through the book of the Acts of the Apostles was the death, burial and resurrection of Jesus Christ. They preach Christ to the lost, not doctrines. These external labels often cloud the church of its true mission to disciple whole communities for Christ. These varying opinions tend to make the church the focus, rather than the kingdom.

If I do not the works of my father, believe me not. But if I do, though ye believe not me, believe the works: that ye may know, and believe, that the Father is in me, and I in him.

John 10:37-38 KJV.

As a consequence of these in-house fightings with each other, we've been busy staying trapped in our religious boxes. We've been locked up in the world of religion at the expense of the other six spheres. Worst yet, we've kept God's people and their unique gifts also trapped and stifled, since we've defined kingdom service as service limited and restricted to the four walls of the church. This makes us one-seventh relevant, and six-sevenths irrelevant. We're losing our saltiness while proudly holding on to our respective crystalline color. But, we're going to have to lose it if we're planning on becoming one with of the world we've been commissioned to disciple. Becoming one here doesn't mean that we conform or compromise with the world, but that we identify with her in a way that allows us to master her culture in order to effectively transform it. It is impossible to change a system we don't understand.

Another point worthy of consideration comes from the understanding that each of the seven spheres are so different from each other. The rules that govern each structure differ from the rules that govern the other structures. To transform the business structure, we would have to understand the rules that govern that world. The rules that govern the world of politics may not fully apply to mass media.

The world is not concerned about external identifications and will never be won over by them. The same principle applies to salt. It is bought and used only because of its power and not for its color. Religious clichés have done more harm than good in turning the world off from Christ. External labeling has done nothing to transform a nation. To win the world, we must lose the shell of all our labels, and return to the simplicity of preaching Christ and Him crucified. The dying world needs to see the gospel in action rather than hearing our claims and opinions.

Jesus had to lose His God-shell, and take on the man-shell. This way He was able to identify with the system He came to change. The usefulness of salt lies in its transformational powers, but once it loses its saltiness or relevance, it is no longer good for anything.

PRINCIPLE FOUR
SALT TAKES ON THE NATURE OF THE SOUP
(IDENTIFY WITH THE SYSTEM TO MASTER IT AND CHANGE IT)

When salt is poured into a pot of soup, it loses its outward shell and takes on the nature of the soup. It actually takes on the nature of whatever it is poured into and not the other way around. This is a very powerful principle: salt takes on the nature of whatever it is poured into and becomes one with it in the same way our Lord Jesus Christ took on the nature of man and became one with man. What does this mean? Christians cannot change a system or structure without identifying with the system first. Jesus became one with the system in order to identify with it and to understand the system. His objective was to transform the system. How can someone change the business sphere with no training in business? To change a system, one must understand how it works. Sitting back and complaining about the entertainment industry is not going to accomplish anything worthwhile, until someone understands it and then seeks to transform it. Too many people have left the political world while hoping and praying that things would change, yet the word of God clearly states that when the righteous are in authority, the people rejoice — Proverb 29:2. The true power of the church takes place as we engage the systems of this world.

IDENTIFYING WITH THE SYSTEMS OF THIS WORLD

Identifying with the world is a necessity, but identification does not mean compromising, nor does it mean conformity. It simply means becoming a master of their systems with the underlining aim to influence it and transform it. It is the training of believers to identify, learn, master, influence and transform the systems of this world. Think about trying to communicate with a foreigner whose language you cannot understand. This would get frustrating. Understanding and speaking the language would establish common grounds for communication. This is what Christians must do in each structure of a nation. For example, if a person is a scientist, they're more likely to relate with and influence a group of scientists.

This is why we desperately need a paradigm shift in our concept of the mission of the church in the bid to disciple nations. Imagine each person in your church being trained to use their lives, their gifts, and their resources to enter, identify, understand, master, influence and transform a sphere or structure. Jesus mastered each sphere in His day and you'd only need to read about His parables to understand how He used the language of His time to communicate His message. He spoke of investment, banking, agriculture, wine-making, fiscal responsibility, the weather, political systems and structures, leadership, responsibility and accountability, work ethic, construction, etc. In fact, none of His disciples were from the religious sector but were all from the marketplace.

PRINCIPLE FIVE
SALT DIES TO LIVE
(SALT IS ALL ABOUT TRANSFORMATIONAL POWER)

It's amazing, isn't it? But salt, like a seed, must die to live. Until salt dissolves into a pot of soup, losing its crystalline shell, like a seed losing its hard shell buried in the earth, the powerful potent life in the salt would not be released to flavor the entire meal. A pinch of salt activates its seasoning power upon death as a drop of ink tinctures a whole glass of water. Salt contains quickening properties.

> **Verily, verily, I say unto you, Except a corn of wheat fall into the ground and die, it abideth alone: but if it die, it bringeth forth much fruit.**
> **John 12:24 KJV**

The point here is that salt contains transformational powers. And this is why we buy and use it to
flavor our meals. The church, too, should be known for
its transformational powers. Our works of transformation in each of the seven structures of society should be
well known. Imagine for a minute what would happen
if the church transformed the educational systems of
this world or the political landscape of the nations of
the earth or the mass media. This is what Jesus meant
when He said that mankind would glorify our Father
in heaven if we would let our light shine. Light illu-
minates, reveals, manifests and displays things. Our
works is how we shine the light of Jesus to the world.
Our lack of works veils Him from the world.

THE UNKNOWN WORK AND MINISTRY OF THE HOLY SPIRIT

Recently, I have felt compelled to write a book on
this aspect of the work and ministry of the Holy Spirit.
The church at large has failed to tap into this vital
work of the Holy Spirit. Her understanding of revival
works of old such as the Welsh and Keswick revival, the
Azusa street revival, the Pensacola revival and others,
have largely contributed to a one-sided form of revival.
Many Christians have held on to these moves of God
as primary or absolute, and unknowingly, closed off
themselves from the "other" potential revivals of God.
It comes from the belief, although traditional, that God

always moves in the same mold of past revivals. First, let me state that I by no means make light of these revivals of old and the similar current ones for they are truly the mighty works of God's Spirit, and have resulted in untold millions coming to Christ. However, an understanding of the Great Commission spoken of in Matthew 28:18-20 clearly reveals that God may be shifting, not revival per say, but the "mode" of revival that will usher in a new relevance for the church of the 21st century.

Obviously, we cannot completely abandon the revivals of old since their biblical patterns have remained consistent from the beginning. However, we should equally and fully embrace all the other modes of revival that are typically not well known, but are, nonetheless, biblical. We're essentially speaking of transformational revivals. Revivals die because of many reasons: one being that we want to enjoy what God is doing but are not willing to truly conform into His likeness. In other words, we lack the character and the lifestyle it takes to sustain a move of God. The objective of all the inner workings of God in the human heart is to make us more like Christ in practice; so that, we can all reveal Him to the world around us. The term "revival" means that something is dying and needs to be resuscitated. Every Christian starts dying when they lose their first love and first works — Rev 2:4-6. If growing in our first love and first works would remain a way of life in the church, there would be no need for revival. Revivals of old tend to have a predictable trend, which is, "What supernaturally comes, supernaturally leaves." Revivals come and leave mainly because it is birthed by the labor of the few, and not everyone is as hungry or as disciplined as the few. Moreover, the motives of many may not be pure because we long to reveal to the world a living Christ via means of a "move," instead of a lifestyle; a way of life as true followers of Jesus Christ. We want God to fix the church and the world through a move of God, rather than through sustained discipleship. Believers were first called Christians at Antioch because they lived like Christ. Apparently, the outpouring of Acts 2 did translate into a way of life. Paul's conversion did not start in Acts 9, but in Acts 7 where he saw Christ's lamb nature in Stephen the martyr, and God used that experience to plow the soil of Paul's heart. Now, let me get to my main point on the theme of this subject.

I would like to introduce another aspect of the work and ministry of the Holy Spirit in building and transforming nations. Let us look at the following scripture:

And the Spirit of the LORD shall rest upon him, the spirit of wisdom and understanding, the spirit of counsel and might, the spirit of knowledge and of the fear of the LORD.

Isaiah 11:2 KJV

These are the seven distinct manifestations of the Holy Spirit, and all of these seven personalities were manifested in Christ. For far too long, we've majored on just one of them — "the spirit of might." It is also known as the "spirit of power or the spirit of strength." This is the aspect of the Holy Spirit that we mostly see in revival meetings and healing conventions. Some actually call these types of meetings, power services. The spirit of might, as in all the other aspects of the Holy Spirit is vitally important, but it is only one-seventh of His features. What about the other six features? Have you noticed that four of them in particular have to do with the operation of the mind? We've embraced one-seventh of His personality, and at the same time neglected four-sevenths of His manifestations. Our relevance in the 21st century will depend on our understanding of these four distinct features of the Holy Spirit — the spirit of wisdom, the spirit of understanding, the spirit of counsel and the spirit of knowledge. All these four specific features, personalities and manifestations of the Holy Spirit have to do with the operation of the mind. Let's use some examples to explain how this works.

First, we see this operation of the Spirit in the life of Bezaleel in Exodus 35:30-35. In verse 31, and it states, "And he hath filled him with the spirit of God, in wisdom, in understanding, and in knowledge, and in all manner of workmanship." This is the work of the Holy Spirit manifesting Himself in wisdom, understanding and knowledge. In verse 32 and 33, it states, "And to devise curious works, to work in gold, and in silver, and in brass, and in the cutting of stones, to set them, and in carving of wood, to make any manner of cunning work. This is the Spirit of God manifesting in skills of craftsmanship. Here, Bezaleel, was empowered by the operation of the Holy Spirit to build the tabernacle of Moses. Therefore, there is an anointing for building, including, the building of whole communities and nations. We see a manifestation of the Holy Spirit in tangible works, in skills for construction, etc. Therefore, wisdom, counsel, understanding and knowledge are all functions of the Holy Spirit operating in and through the human mind for transformational purposes.

These functions, however, operate within the shrine of man's born-again spirit, while simultaneously influencing and illuminating the mind. The sole objective here is to transform our thought-processes from which divine concepts and creative ideas are born. An example of this would be a miraculous healing of cancer where the prayer of faith was offered for someone or where the gifts of healings were in full operation manifesting the healing of a disease. The church at large would rejoice over such a powerful, supernatural, and miraculous manifestation of the Holy Spirit, and rightfully so. But how come we've never believed God for the operation of the same Spirit in the area of science and medicine to find a cure for cancer? Because of our traditional views on healing, we've limited God and His manifestations in other fields. Can you imagine if the cure for cancer were in the hands of the church in both a supernatural and scientific sense! It would restore her relevance overnight, and open up unbelievable opportunities for the church to advance the cause of Christ in the earth.

It amazes me sometimes how childish we've become even in spiritual matters. Our understanding of the anointing is mostly falling under the power, shaking, screaming, shouting and all the other bodily sensations. I don't think there's anything essentially wrong with such manifestations of the Spirit since I have personally experienced so many of such manifestations. However, take a good look at some nations in the world where there's a strong emphasis on the work of the Holy Spirit and yet, they lack the necessary skill sets to build and sustain a basic infrastructure. Most African nations would qualify as an example for the above illustration and yet, there's still a strong presence of systemic corruption and systemic poverty on every level imaginable. The anointing they exhibit within their four walls has not done much to improve their environmental or educational or social-economic or political structures. Meanwhile, Singapore, a nation of many religions has an extremely notable presence of law and order and one of the best infrastructures in the world. They achieved this through vision, strong ethics, tested character, fairness and equity, national discipline and faith in the impossible, considering that they were a third world nation three decades years ago. To remain relevant, we must embrace a paradigm shift in our understanding of the anointing. It is the manifestation of God in providing cures for societal ills and enhancing the value of life in a nation as a whole. Remember that scripture again, "And he hath filled him with the spirit of God in wisdom, and in knowledge, and in understanding, and in all manner of workman-ship — Exodus 35:31.

The second example would be Joseph, the son of Jacob. The scripture states, "And Pharaoh said unto his servants, can we find such a one as this in whom the Spirit of God is?" – Genesis 41:38. In what specific way did Pharoah, a heathen king, observe the operation of the Spirit through Joseph? He saw God's Spirit at work in Joseph through his ability to interpret dreams, and through Joseph's ability to provide creative solu-tions to a national crisis – Gen 41:33-36. The question we should all ask still is how was Joseph able to build storages to hold perishable food for thirteen years in a land known for extremely hot climates, and without any refrigeration? He did it through the anointing of God's Spirit manifesting in wisdom, understanding and knowledge, leading to national transformation.

In conclusion, we should learn from the Israel of old who through their ignorance of God and His works, failed to enter into their promised land, in spite of all the miracles they saw and experienced. They had become so dependent on their view of the miraculous that their minds never fully developed. Like babies, they constantly waited for manna from heaven without developing life skills – a necessity for life on earth. God never meant for the gifts of the Spirit to substitute the cultivation of skills, and this was a major part of the reason why the miracles had to cease when they entered into Canaan. God told them to apply themselves to working the fields, and in the process, to develop skills for building a nation. In today's church, our views of the anointing should embrace the whole counsel of God, and especially the fourfold anointing of the Spirit relative to the functions of the mind. Thinkers rule the world and workers will always remain their slaves.

Allow God to move in your mind and illuminate it with ideas for transforming your world. Have you noticed that in most African churches, the things we constantly ask God for, most of the developed world, without God, have them? Why? Because the earth is made up of laws and those laws are unwavering and unchanging and know no race, creed, color, gender or religion. Those laws are not prejudiced or biased and they show no favoritism. In all of our getting, it's time to acquire understanding. We should earnestly seek God's ways instead of His acts always — Psalms 103:7. Since the economic crisis of 2008, what solutions, and I mean precise and applicable ones, has the body of Christ provided to governmental leaders? Has the world felt our influence and impact in this area? Where are the Josephs of this generation?

PRINCIPLE SIX
SALT PERMEATES THE ENTIRE SOUP
(THE WISDOM OF GOD CAUSING NOISELESS IMPACT)

**But as truly as I live, all the earth shall
be filled with the glory of the Lord.**
Numbers 14:21 KJV

God wants the whole world filled and saturated with His glory. The desire to fill the earth with His glory is an extremely important kingdom business. God desires that this present evil world be progressively overtaken by the rule and reign of His government. This all-encompassing desire is the heart of the Great Commission.

I remember returning from Japan in 2008 after a two-week trip to Tokyo and Osaka. It was from that trip that the inspiration to write this book was first developed.

I came home, and a strong anointing from the Holy Spirit fell on me for weeks. During those weeks, I had a personal encounter with God that would change my life forever, and ushered me into my international ministry called "transformation of nations." In three years, I had travelled to over 40 nations, and many of those nations, ten to thirteen times over. It was out of that encounter that I got the opportunity to speak with different government parliaments, and some heads of state and their cabinets, and thousands of students on how to transform their nation. In that encounter from Japan, God made me take personal responsibility for advancing His kingdom throughout the earth.

DANIEL'S SPEAKS OF GOD'S GLORY
FILLING THE EARTH

Thou, O king, sawest, and behold a great image. This great image, whose brightness was excellent, stood before thee; and the form thereof was terrible. This image's head was of fine gold, his breast and his arms of silver, his belly and his thighs of brass, His legs of iron, his feet part of iron and part of clay. Thou sawest till that a stone was cut out without hands, which smote the image upon his feet that were of iron and clay, and brake them to pieces. Then was the iron, the clay, the brass, the silver, and the gold, broken to pieces together, and became like the chaff of the summer threshingfloors; and the wind carried them away, that no place was found for them: and the stone that smote the image became a great mountain, and filled the whole earth.

And in the days of these kings shall the God of heaven set up a kingdom, which shall never be destroyed: and the kingdom shall not be left to other people, but it shall break in pieces and consume all these kingdoms, and it shall stand for ever. Forasmuch as thou sawest that the stone was cut out of the mountain without hands, and that it brake in pieces the iron, the brass, the clay, the silver, and the gold; the great God hath made known to the king what shall come to pass hereafter: and the dream is certain, and the interpretation thereof sure.

Daniel 2:31-35, 44-45 KJV

So, you see that God's vision is to completely displace the kingdoms of this world from the face of the earth, and replace it with the kingdom of His dear son, Jesus.

It is only through the understanding of the Great Commission can we achieve God's dream of filling the earth with the glory of God. The book of revelation states that the kingdoms of this world shall become the kingdom of God, and of His Christ — Revelation 11:15.

When salt is poured into a pot of soup, its subtlety infiltrates the entire pot of soup. It only takes a pinch of salt to saturate an entire pot of soup. Salt reaches saturation at 26.4% per room temperature, which means that it would take some considerable

time to properly place God's people into a system to help transform it from the inside out. However, the work of training the saints to penetrate systems and structures, strategically is worth the wait. Great patience must be exercised intentionally. The wisdom lies in this patience. Salt penetrates the entire soup in a noiseless fashion.

DEVELOPING A LONGTERM FOCUSED STRATEGY

It's only within Christendom, that we've failed to develop a long-term strategy to fulfilling the mandate of the Great Commission. The church, God's body, in the earth, is so fragmented on so many levels that it lacks strategy: that's a long term focused concerted effort to achieving kingdom goals. Every local body has a sepa-rate agenda from another body with no clear end-goal. The goal is not a shared goal driven by a shared effort in the body. It seems like every member of the body is simply doing their own "thing." We lack a global agenda for world evangelization. Surely, our power lies in our unity with a unified objective. The majority of us in Christ can agree on the call to evangelize the world as God's most important corporate assignment given to the body. This corporate assignment known as the Great Commission, should at least trump our personal idiosyncrasies, causing the light of His gospel to shine brightest through a unified effort.

> **Behold, how good and how pleasant it is for brethren to dwell together in unity! It is like the precious ointment upon the head, that ran down upon the beard, even Aaron's beard: that went down to the skirts of his garments; As the dew of Hermon, and as the dew that descended upon the mountains of Zion: for there the Lord commanded the blessing, even life for evermore.**
> **Psalm 133:1-3 KJV**

God's church has no single plan in place that's understood by its body. We've been shooting too many arrows in too many different directions hoping to reach the same goal. We need to live out each day with an overarching consciousnesses of God's corporate assignment for His church. This one goal ought to be the lifeblood of the church — the one thing that drives us all; the one thing we all revolve our lives around. It should be the central vision of the church. It should be our creed. Every true believer on the planet should have the blueprint for fulfilling the Great Commission. In North Korea, they have their Ten Commandments, which every citizen must memorize from birth. In the same way, every believer born into the kingdom should memorize the kingdom creed, and fully understand the Great Commission's long-term plan to evangelizing the world. We need to work in a strategic way, and with a concerted effort toward this goal. This is that wisdom needed to fill the earth with the glory of God.

> **And he by his wisdom delivered the city ... then said I, wisdom is better than strength.**
> **Ecclesiastes 9:14-16 KJV**

The church needs God's wisdom displayed in its various forms in these last days. We need intelligent strategic minds on the drawing board. We need wise people who know how to develop a clear blueprint and lead the church with focused determination toward that goal. Instead of expending way too much energy and resources spread in a thousand different directions with little to no results, we can harness our abilities and pull our resources in a concerted effort and strike a big blow. Think about buying CNN or NBC or Fox outrightly or as the majority shareholder and use it as a major platform to proclaim the gospel. Wisdom, indeed, will always be the principal thing.

PRINCIPLE SEVEN
SALT TRANSFORMS THE ENTIRE SOUP
(SALT TRANSFORMS ANYTHING IT TOUCHES AT A CELLULAR LEVEL, IRREVERSIBLY)

Imagine the impact the church would have on the world if we trained God's people with intentionality, raising them up to penetrate the systems of this world, and transforming it with the values of the kingdom of God. We need one vision: the Great Commission vision. If we divided each local church into seven parts, each part intentionally trained to address a specific sphere, we would find ourselves making a huge impact for God's kingdom.

> **You shall describe the land in seven divisions, and bring the description here to me. I will cast lots for you here before the Lord our God.**
>
> **Joshua 18:6 AMP**

Each sphere contains sub-spheres. So, there's so much to teach or disciple God's people into. There's also much room for all to participate in, while using their time, talents and treasures toward addressing a specific sphere or sub-sphere. As already stated, filling each sphere with the value system of the kingdom of God helps to prime a nation for revival; sustained revival. South Korea, a third world nation in the 1950's, through a sustained revival, became one of the most developed nations in the world. I was personally blown away by their level of development when I visited in 2010, considering they were the second poorest nation in the world, and second only to Somalia, sixty years prior. By the time I visited, that revival had been going on for thirty-five to forty years transforming the landscape of South Korea through the church. Sustained revival is the result of sustained discipleship. We need a strategic blueprint on how to have a sustained move of God that literally transforms every single sphere of a nation. We need a sustained move of God that inspires people to live a life of significance for God.

Salt affects things on a cellular level. At a cellular level, things remain irreversible. Sustained change happens at a cellular level. This is that level where things change irreversibly. I believe in a measurable impact, which helps us see the work that has been done, and the work that has to be done. But real change requires that we gain grounds in a progressive way.

The Spirit of the Lord God is upon me; because the Lord hath anointed me to preach good tidings unto the meek; he hath sent me to bind up the brokenhearted, to proclaim liberty to the captives, and the opening of the prison to them that are bound; To proclaim the acceptable year of the Lord, and the day of vengeance of our God; to comfort all that mourn; To appoint unto them that mourn in Zion, to give unto them beauty for ashes, the oil of joy for mourning, the garment of praise for the spirit of

heaviness; that they might be called trees of righteousness, the planting of the Lord, that he might be glorified. And they shall build the old wastes, they shall raise up the former desolations, and they shall repair the waste cities, the desolations of many generations.
Isaiah 61:1-4 KJV

A huge part of God's anointing on our lives has to do with becoming the trees of righteousness, the planting of the Lord. We're are to become a stable and sustainable force in the earth. Only then can we build the old wastes, and raise up the former desolations.

Chapter 4:

THE TWO MAIN FUNCTIONS OF SALT
"KINGDOM RESPONSIBILITIES OF A BELIEVER"

For unto us a child is born, unto us a son is given: and the government shall be upon his shoulder: and his name shall be called Wonderful, Counsellor, The mighty God, The everlasting Father, The Prince of Peace. Of the increase of his government and peace there shall be no end, upon the throne of David, and upon his kingdom, to order it, and to establish it with judgment and with justice from henceforth even forever. The zeal of the Lord of hosts will perform this.

Isaiah 9:6-7 KJV

The government of God shall rest upon our shoulders. We are to bear the responsibility of spreading the influence of the kingdom of God around the world.

Each of us should take this responsibility extremely personal. There can be no single delay or procrastination from any of us from fully stepping into the call to disciple the nations of the earth. We should all embrace it as if it all depended upon our singular responsive action. Let's trust God that by His mighty Spirit there would be an unceasing weighty burden eternally infused into our soul for this kingdom responsibility. Only by the flames of God's Spirit shall we burn with the burden of the Lord. There shall be no end to the increase of God's kingdom; no, not in this world or in the worlds to come. His reign shall be forever limitless.

UNTO US A CHILD IS BORN; UNTO US A SON IS GIVEN

When the Lord fully revealed this Scripture to me in a prayer encounter, He showed me that I was born for the nations, and that I would be given to the nations as a gift from God. He showed me that until I was ready to take personal responsibility for the transformation of the nations that this anointing would not come upon me. In that encounter, I heard the nations calling me to come to their aid like Paul, the Apostle did in a vision.

And a vision appeared to Paul in the night; There stood a man of Macedonia,

and prayed him, saying, Come over into Macedonia, and help us.

Acts 16:9 KJV

Whether you realize it or not, you were born for a nation. And the nation connected to your destiny is calling out to you night and day to answer the call. Can you hear the sound? Can you hear the sigh and the groaning of the people? Creation calls at you to take responsibility for her. The more you grow into your sonship, the more responsibility you'll have. We're each born for a people as saviors (Obadiah 1:21), and as deliverers (Exodus 3:10), and prophets (Jeremiah 1:5), but we're only given to the world as sons (John 3:16).

For unto you is born this day in the City of David a savior, which is Christ the Lord

Luke 2:11 KJV.

The Father calls us and sends us out in the same way He called Jesus, His firstborn son, and sent Him out. Jesus said, "As the Father sent me into the world, even so have I also sent you into the world" — John 17:18 KJV.

For though I preach the gospel, I have nothing to glory of: for necessity is laid upon me; yea, woe is unto me, if I

preach not the gospel! For if I do this thing willingly, I have a reward: but if against my will, a dispensation of the gospel is committed unto me.

1 Corinthians 9:16-17 KJV

Paul, the Apostle, was used mightily by God and perhaps, arguably, as the greatest Apostle that ever lived. A dispensation of the gospel was committed to him, and he faithfully delivered on that assignment until his death. He wholeheartedly accepted that responsibility as the man who could deliver it best, and as though it depended only on him to do it. And in a sense, it did. We, too, have to take responsibility for our communities and nations, as though it only depended on us, and only then, would God give us His backing. Like Moses, the man of God, we need to move forward and stretch out our rods over the Red Sea.

FAITH FOR NATIONS

Ask of me, and I shall give thee the heathen for thine inheritance, and the uttermost parts of the earth for thy possession

Psalm 2:8 KJV

The sons of God are far more concerned with possessing territories for Jesus. They are consumed with filling the earth with the glory of God. They are mission-minded.

They may start out in their respective Jerusalem, but their goal is to possess the ends of the earth. The increase of God's government in the earth, also known as the Great Commission, is the one thing that drives all their actions in life. We need the faith that takes nations for Jesus.

> **For I am the Lord thy God, the Holy One of Israel, thy Saviour: I gave Egypt for thy ransom, Ethiopia and Seba for thee. Since thou wast precious in my sight, thou hast been honourable, and I have loved thee: therefore will I give men for thee, and people for thy life. Fear not: for I am with thee: I will bring thy seed from the east, and gather thee from the west; I will say to the north, Give up; and to the south, Keep not back: bring my sons from far, and my daughters from the ends of the earth;**
>
> **Isaiah 43:3-6 KJV**

God is so ready to give up the nations for your sake. He is so ready to deliver Egypt, Ethiopia and all the nations of the earth, and to call our sons and daughters back home from the ends of the earth. But someone has to respond to the call, and step in to take responsibility. Let's release our faith and believe God for entire nations to be saved — Revelation 21:24. Let God's people like salt saturate the world with the flavor of righteousness, peace and joy.

PRESERVING LIVES FROM DECADENCE

Salt acts as a preserving agent; as an anti-microbial control agent it suppresses the growth of spoilage organisms. It preserves certain proteins such as meat and fish from decaying by controlling fermentation and by slowing down the decaying process.

> **For God sent me ahead of you to preserve life**
> **Genesis 45:5 AMP**

God is sending us ahead of the rest to help preserve lives. This is why God would raise someone in a family to lead the rest out of bondage into freedom. We've been called to call others out. We've been raised to raise others up. We've been blessed to bless the families of the earth. We preserve lives by fully embracing the call of the Great Commission.

HOW DO WE PRESERVE LIVES?

We'll better understand how to preserve lives by understanding how Satan destroys lives. The Bible shows us how Satan destroys lives and nations in both the Old and New Testament. In the book of Isaiah, Satan is identified as the one who weakens the nations.

How art thou fallen from heaven, O Lucifer, son of the morning! how art thou cut down to the ground, which didst weaken the nations!

Isaiah 14:12 KJV

And how exactly does Satan weaken the nations? In the book of Daniel, and in Revelation, the Bible tells us with the most assuredly clarity how he accomplishes this.

And whereas thou sawest the feet and toes, part of potters' clay, and part of iron, the kingdom shall be divided; but there shall be in it of the strength of the iron, forasmuch as thou sawest the iron mixed with miry clay. And as the toes of the feet were part of iron, and part of clay, so the kingdom shall be partly strong, and partly broken. And whereas thou sawest iron mixed with miry clay, they shall mingle themselves with the seed of men: but they shall not

**cleave one to another, even as iron is
not mixed with clay.**

Daniel 2:41-43 KJV

We see Satan, the potter, pottering the clay. The clay symbolizes the ejection of a depraved value system designed to displace God from society. In this context, it's an immoral value system whose main objective is to destroy the biblical establishment of the marriage institution. It's a satanic attack levied at the roots of the family institution, the source and foundation of all civilization. Displace the family unit, and you displace a nation. By destroying the moral fiber of a nation, you open the floodgates for all manner of unclean demonic spirits into a society with no restraint to what's wrong or right. Here, truth becomes relative, rather than absolute.

WHAT'S HIS STRATEGY?

**And there came one of the seven angels
which had the seven vials, and talked
with me, saying unto me, Come hither;
I will shew unto thee the judgment
of the great whore that sitteth upon
many waters: With whom the kings of
the earth have committed fornication,
and the inhabitants of the earth have**

been made drunk with the wine of her fornication.

Revelation 17:1-2 KJV

Satan goes after the authorities in position of power. He goes after the kings. And this is why the Bible admonishes us to pray for all who are in authority so that we can live tranquil lives — 1 Timothy 2:1-4. He goes after the authorities because it is the easiest way to get to the people. First, you capture and control the leadership, then, you take control of her people. In other words, you strike the shepherd and scatter the sheep, or you bind the strong man and spoil his house. The goal is to bring both the kings of the nations of the earth and her citizens under the spell of Satan — 1 John 5:19. I know many may think that this is impossible, but history is our best witness here. Satan uses demonic doctrines to create belief systems evolving into a "new culture." He gives the leaders: the executive, legislative and judiciary arms of the government a philosophy of life, and passes these beliefs systems through established policies and laws for the people to live by them. This is how he changes the culture priming it for all forms of demonic activity. Here, you'll notice that with this change, the cultural atmosphere becomes pervasively antagonistic to all things pertaining to the God of the Bible. The goal as previously stated is to remove the consciousness of God from society. It was no coincidence that the DNC under Obama's presidency, publicly and unanimously voted God out of the nation. When we vote God out of anything, then by inference, we invite Satan in. Prayer and Bible study became unconstitutional in schools across America. Demonic doctrines on neutral-gender lifestyles were being taught in our primary and elementary schools with government approved curricula. So many people fell for it, and most of the church became both intimidated and silenced.

So, we preserve lives by keeping the cultural environment primed for the gospel. Righteousness exalts a nation, but sin is a reproach to any people — Proverbs 14:34. We preserve lives by filling the earth with the knowledge of God. We must keep the value systems of the kingdom of God alive in all the seven structures upon which every society of people are formed. A huge part of advancing the kingdom of God in the earth comes from advancing His value systems in the society. Atmosphere is critical to the success of the gospel — Ephesians 2:2; 2 Thessalonians 3:1. Nations such as Japan, North Korea, India, all of Northern Africa, and what is known as the 10-40 window nations, have become major strongholds for the propagation of the gospel. This satanic stronghold is mostly both cultural and atmospheric.

RIGHTLY POSITIONING GOD'S PEOPLE TO ENGAGE THE CULTURE OF OUR TIMES

It is important that the church rightfully positions God's people to excel in their respective fields of endeavor. As children of the King of kings, we should be the best in our field as a means to establishing God's kingdom in the earth. Training and education are vital to natural and spiritual success. Connect your assignment to one or more of the seven structures of society. For example, are you called to the business sector or educational sector? What areas within the educational system do you intend to change? Define it with the ultimate goal of displacing world systems with kingdom values. Plan, strategize, and get a working blueprint. It must go beyond treating symptoms to curing root causes. Find like-minded people who share the same passion and work together as a team.

> **Now after that John was put in prison, Jesus came into Galilee, preaching the gospel of the kingdom of God, And saying, The time is fulfilled, and the kingdom of God is at hand: repent ye, and believe the gospel.**
>
> **Mark 1:14-15 KJV**

Jesus preached and practiced the gospel of the kingdom of God three and a half years before a single person became born again. No one could be saved or become born again until Jesus rose from the dead. In His message, He told the masses to change their way of thinking — a radical turn from the existing culture of the day. The gospel of the kingdom is the message of the reign, the rule or the government of God super-imposed upon the kingdoms of this world. Jesus came to reintroduce the culture of heaven into the earth. He had to prime the people and the nations of the earth through a progressive establishment of the reign of the government of God. The more godless a society becomes, the more difficult and hardened the soil where the seed of the gospel can thrive. They've told us that the seed determines the harvest, but this not entirely true. It is the soil and the seed that determines it, but primarily, it's the soil. Filling the earth with the value systems of the kingdom of God helps to prime the atmosphere for the seed of the gospel of Jesus Christ to thrive in the earth. In other words, the gospel of the Lord Jesus thrives on the foundation of the gospel of the kingdom of God. It took Jesus three and a half years to prep the soil for the gospel. A soil can become so contaminated like that of Noah's generation or of Sodom and Gomorrah, that God would have to completely destroy it and start all over again. What use is a seed if there's no soil to place it in? No matter how powerful the seed to produce, it is powerless without the soil. The essential call to disciple the nations of the earth is to prime the soil for the success of the gospel of the Lord Jesus Christ into the hearts of men, and into society.

FLAVORING THE WORLD WITH THE VALUES OF THE KINGDOM

The second primary function of salt is for flavoring our meals. Salt not only seasons food but also suppresses other taste responses such as sweet, sour, and bitter. This salt additive has a functional factor in modifying food through a complex chemical reaction that provides a desirable finished product. Salt can give taste to a meal and make it desirable.

> **Can that which is unsavoury be eaten without salt? or is there any taste in the white of an egg?**
>
> **Job 6:6 KJV**

Believers all over the world are to flavor all the seven spheres of society with the value systems of the kingdom of God. The world can become quite a tasteless place. Clearly, a world without Jesus is an empty world, full of vanities. But I wished that believers would become more tasteful in their souls, and in their dispositions. We ought to be the ones giving the world enough reasons to turn to Christ. We ought to bring to the table some serious flavor people! Our joy and fun in serving God ought to be so contagious and extremely attractive.

If we act like the world and live like the world, then why should the world be interested in us or in who we claim to be representing? If am always depressed like the world; always broken, beaten, battered and shattered; always unhappy and full of sorry stories, why would the world want any of that? If am always defeated and always struggling with addictions, why would anyone want my life? We would need to finally come face to face with the truth: does the gospel of Jesus Christ radically transform lives or not? Does it contain the power of turning us into new creatures whose new DNA strands are filled with attractive attributes? Does His gospel and His life make us vividly distinct from the rest of the world or not? Are Christians simply sick folks living permanently in a hospital hoping just to get a little bit better? I've said this before: it is practically impossible to live right if one's theology is wrong. And I am concerned that many Christians are having a very hard time living victoriously because their theology was built on a faulty foundation. Jesus said: "you are the salt of the earth." That's who you are. It's in you to flavor your world. You give the world its taste. You give it its sense. You make it all make sense. You're the missing ingredient in the pot that brings it altogether. You're the center where all the puzzles of life finally connect to give meaning to the bigger picture.

We have become the unmistakable aroma of the victory of the Anointed One

to God —a perfume of life to those being saved and the odor of death to those who are perishing. The unbelievers smell a deadly stench that leads to death, but believers smell the life-giving aroma that leads to abundant life. And who of us can rise to this challenge?

2 Corinthians 2:15-16 TPT

The life of our loving Savior radically transforms the human heart, and fundamentally impacts one's lifestyle resulting into a vivid distinction between his new life and old life. Such a change is so prevalent and visible that it literally causes an immediate divide between the bearer and his old friends. It will either cause a friend to turn to the Lord or completely stay away; but, there are usually no middle grounds or grey areas for a third option. Here, as the Scriptures above point out, we become a sweet fragrance among the saved or a stench among the dead. And this fragrance best expresses itself through the nature, character and the attributes of Jesus Christ. Like salt, the seasoning in itself are the values of the kingdom of God. We flavor the world with these values.

His son is the reflection of God's glory and the exact likeness of God's being

Hebrews 1:3 GWT

If people really got to know the real Jesus, they'll either love Him or hate Him, but they won't be any middle grounds. His life forces one to change or to completely turn away. And through us, we're able to put Him on display 24/7 for all the world to see. For as He is, so are we in this world — 1 John 4:18.

Chapter 5

HINDRANCES TO A SALTED LIFE
"KINGDOM CHARACTER AND KINGDOM VALUES"

"Value-systems without Christ are not only unattainable but impossible"
–Sino Agueze

You are like salt for the whole human race. But if salt loses its saltiness, there is no way to make it salty again. It has become worthless, so it is thrown out and people trample on it.
Matthew 5:13 GNT

D id you know that Jesus used the above state-ment in three different incidents at three dif-ferent places at three different times to three different audiences? This statement ties into the three hin-drances to living a salted life. The second hindrance is found in the Gospel of Matthew 5, popularly known as the beatitudes of Christ, and is considered till date the greatest message preached to humanity. The "Beatitudes" are the strongest expression of the values of the kingdom of God. The third hindrance is found in the Gospel of Mark 9, and is known as the self-sabotage character traits. These traits identify those who betray Christ by their lifestyle.

UNDERSTANDING THE BEATITUDES AS THE VALUES OF GOD'S KINGDOM

The beatitudes define the character of the King and His kingdom. They collectively represent the culture of God's domain. If you've ever asked or you're not certain what the value system of God's kingdom is — it is fully summed up in the beatitudes. These are attitudes we import into all the seven spheres of the systems of the world. They are attitudes we must develop in our own lives as a means to revealing a counter-culture to the culture of this world because God's culture is dramatically opposed to the culture of the spirit of this world.

BEATITUDE ONE

Blessed are the poor in spirit: for theirs is the kingdom of heaven.

Matthew 5:3 KJV

**Spiritually prosperous are the destitute
and helpless in the realm of the spirit,
because theirs is the kingdom of heaven.**
Mathew 5:3 WENT

The first beatitude says blessed are the poor in spirit for theirs is the kingdom of heaven. Jesus was not talking about financial poverty because someone who is poor can be just as mean, in sin and ungodly as anyone else. The meaning of this word "poor" in the Greek means one who sees himself or herself as nothing or as bankrupt without God. It is abject poverty, utter helplessness, and complete destitution, subsisting on the alms of others without God. It paints the picture of the beggar at the beautiful gate, crippled from birth and needing the least assistance just to survive — Acts 3:2.

The poor in spirit are those who understand that they are nothing apart from God. The world teaches us, in a very subtle way, that our value and worth are found in things outside of ourselves: what type of family we come from, our education, our physical appearance, our career, our wealth etc. There is nothing intrinsically wrong with any of these things, but if they are the source of our value and worth, we are in trouble. There is always someone who is more attractive, smarter, in a higher position, more educated, or wealthier, and all of these things can be taken away in a moment.

Believers must recognize and embrace this poverty of spirit. Even Jesus, who was anointed without measure said, "The son can do nothing of himself" (John 5:19); "I can of mine own self do nothing" (John 5:30); "My doctrine is not mine, but his that sent me" (John 7:16); "For I have not spoken of myself" (John 12:49)." Jesus repeatedly acknowledged that He was fully dependent on the Father rather than on Himself. Anything that stems from self lacks the carrying power in the kingdom of God because it is concerned with its own interest, and not that of the Father's. When believers take on the attitude of being poor in spirit, they are able to see their own spiritual destitution without God.

> **You're blessed when you're at the end of your rope; with less of you, there is more of God and His rule.**
>
> **Matthew 5:3 MSG**

Imagine for a minute the sheer impact of God's Spirit upon a soul that has intentionally chosen to live completely dependent on God. I love King Solomon's example. He called himself a child who lacked the least capacity for self-direction. He desperately needed God's guidance for every single move he made in life, and for every single decision he made in judging the people of Israel. Such a stance made him a powerhouse in the kingdom of God, and the whole world sought to his wisdom.

Let's become that dependent on God in keeping with staying poor in spirit. The less of us, the more of Him.

MY PERSONAL EXPERIENCE IN BRAZIL

I had traveled to Brazil in April 2015 upon a direct instruction from the Holy Spirit after a twenty-one day fast. The minute I got on the aircraft, God spoke to me to go on an additional fast, and not to eat anything. He told me that He was going to teach me something during the fast, and that I was to pay the utmost attention to what He was going to be showing me. At a conference in Brazil, I had preached Friday, all day and Saturday. The meeting in my estimation on the first two days was powerful — very powerful or so I thought. I had rested in on Sunday morning, and was getting ready for my fifth meeting that Sunday night. I was seated in front when I arrived at the already packed meeting, and in a few minutes after, while the worship was in high gear, I fell into a trance. In that trance, I was caught up to the third heaven, and had no idea what was going on in the meeting. I knew God was dealing with me in a very powerful way, but at that moment, I had no idea why. All I remember was I couldn't stop sobbing like a little child and was feeling a little embarrassed as a part of my consciousness returned. I pleaded with God not to publicly embarrass me in front of everyone, but I simply couldn't stop sobbing. The person close to me had tapped me and indicated that I had been called

up to the podium to speak. I didn't hear them introduce me or call me up. When I got up to the podium, I
immediately went down on my knees, and further went
completely down on my face. Right there fully pros-
trated on the floor, I could at once design that there
was a glorious presence standing right over my head. I
knew it was the Lord Jesus Christ, and I was so afraid
to stretch out my arms in fear that I would be grabbing
both of His feet. Suddenly, words not from this world,
although in English, were given to me by the Holy Spirit,
and I heard myself calling Jesus like a lover would call
for his love. I called Him my darling, sweetheart, lover,
king, etc. I couldn't stop telling Him how much I loved
Him. I was told that I had been on the floor for about
thirty minutes, although, it only felt like a moment.
On that floor, some powerful and life changing events
were all happening simultaneously. I felt powerful volts
of electricity running throughout my entire being. At
this time, a holy hush had enveloped the entire audito-
rium. You could hear a pin drop. Then the Lord spoke
to me and said that He was going to take one hundred
percent control of my entire being, including my fac-
ulties. He said that no part of me would be left to me
except my conscious mind. He told me that the reason
why He would fully possess all parts of me except my
conscious mind was so that I would be able to observe
how He was going to use me that night. He told me
to pay attention. Right after that conversation, I got
up and asked the Lord if I was to step down from the

podium and take back my seat or if He had any other instruction for me. He then told me to give the message I had prepared for the evening. It was a teaching on Ezekiel 47 — a teaching on the four levels of the Spirit. I noticed that my entire being felt like a leaf flowing in the hand of the wind. I felt being borne along by the Holy Spirit's choosing. I wasn't expounding the Scriptures or giving an exposition on the Scriptures. I wasn't teaching or revealing the Scriptures. Not a single self-effort was being exerted in speaking or in explaining the Scriptures. It was completely effortless as though someone else was unpremeditatedly speaking through me. Every word was being directly dictated to me, and simultaneously placed in my mouth to speak at the Spirit's pace. I had noticed that in some unexplainable way, my spirit entered into a mystic union with each person present, and I at once, knew their past, present and future. God was using my brokenness to break all who were present. That meeting started at eight but didn't finish till about 2am. I had called their problems out through the manifestation of the gifts of the Spirit but as though I was right there when it happened. The cases that were called out were far too detailed, and not a single soul in that meeting was weary or tired. God had enveloped the entire building with His presence. It was in that meeting that God revealed that the pastor and his wife were going to have a baby one year from then since they have been expecting one for years now. And they did have a beautiful daughter a year later. At the end of this experience, God said to me that this is how He wants to use me at all times. This is how He wants to possess us all at all times, hallelujah!

BEATITUDE TWO

Blessed are they that mourn: for they shall be comforted
Matthew 5:4 KJV.

The second beatitude is a rare virtue in today's world. Those who mourn according to this beatitude are not mourning from a natural standpoint, i.e. mourning as an emotional response to loss or death. The mourning Jesus is talking about is a spiritual mourning over spiritual matters. Here, believers who realize their spiritual need and poverty, when they examine themselves in the light of God's word and God's standard, they mourn. People can mourn over their own lives, mourn over the lives of others who fail or fall short, mourn over the church when abuse of the grace of God is evident, etc. Jesus wept over Israel when she rejected God and killed her prophets. Even today it is possible to believe He still weeps over the state of the church, with so many people living beneath their rights and privileges in Christ. One can spiritually mourn over the world when they see how many people are under the cruel oppression of the devil. The psalmist himself mourned over the sins of God's people — "Tears stream down from my eyes, because they do not keep your law" Psalms 119:136.

Those who mourn do not rejoice at the fall or mishaps of others.

They wail at the sinful state of a nation and its damaging effects on its people, resources and the land. It is with righteous grief they cry out in intercession for God's mercy to prevail over judgment (2 Corinthians 12:21). These are people who have great faith in God and wholeheartedly believe that their persistence in prayer will procure God's intervention in the lives and circumstances of a people.

KING DAVID'S EXAMPLE

> **And they mourned, and wept, and fasted until even, for Saul, and for Jonathan his son, and for the people of the LORD, and for the house of Israel; because they were fallen by the sword**
>
> **2 Samuel 1:12 KJV**

King Saul made David's life a living hell. He attempted three separate times to murder him. In short, Saul, David's archenemy, had only one objective in mind: and that was to completely obliterate David from the face of the earth. It is no wonder that David was called a man after God's own heart. In-spite of all the inhumane treatments and unbearable mistreatments and vicious hostility suffered at the hand of king Saul, David, on hearing of the death of the king, mourned for him, and spoke so highly and kindly of him as he wept bitterly for him.

And David lamented with this lamentation over Saul and over Jonathan his son: (Also he bade them teach the children of Judah the use of the bow: behold, it is written in the book of Jasher.) The beauty of Israel is slain upon thy high places: how are the mighty fallen! Tell it not in Gath, publish it not in the streets of Askelon; lest the daughters of the Philistines rejoice, lest the daughters of the uncircumcised triumph. Ye mountains of Gilboa, let there be no dew, neither let there be rain, upon you, nor fields of offerings: for there the shield of the mighty is vilely cast away, the shield of Saul, as though he had not been anointed with oil. From the blood of the slain, from the fat of the mighty, the bow of Jonathan turned not back, and the sword of Saul returned not empty. Saul and Jonathan were lovely and pleasant in their lives, and in their death they were not divided: they were swifter

than eagles, they were stronger than lions. Ye daughters of Israel, weep over Saul, who clothed you in scarlet, with other delights, who put on ornaments of gold upon your apparel. How are the mighty fallen in the midst of the battle! O Jonathan, thou wast slain in thine high places. I am distressed for thee, my brother Jonathan: very pleasant hast thou been unto me: thy love to me was wonderful, passing the love of women. How are the mighty fallen, and the weapons of war perished!

2 Samuel 1:17-27 KJV

Those who mourn, even for their enemies, are truly Christ-like in nature. Notice how David sang Saul's praise and how he never uttered a single negative word against him or talked about the trauma and pain he suffered at the hand of king Saul. He didn't go rejoicing at his death or thanked God for finally judging the one person standing between him and the promised throne. The "mourning" beatitude was a part of his gracious nature (2 Samuel 4:1-12). The body of Christ should never hand over their brothers and sisters to the enemy and hang them out to dry like the Israelites handed out Samson to the Philistines (Judges 15:11-13). They should pour out their hearts to God and intercede for mercy and restoration and mourning for those who fall.

At the same token, believers should also be concerned about the spiritual, moral and material state of a people.

> **And when he was come near, he beheld the city, and wept over it, Saying, If thou hadst known, even thou, at least in this thy day, the things which belong unto thy peace! But now they are hid from thine eyes. For the days shall come upon thee, that thine enemies shall cast a trench about thee, and compass thee round, and keep thee in on every side, And shall lay thee even with the ground, and thy children within thee; and they shall not leave in thee one stone upon another; because thou knewest not the time of thy visitation.**
>
> **Luke 19:41-44 KJV**

Jesus mourned for the spiritual blindness of Israel in failing to recognize her true Messiah, and for the consequences that would befall them as a result of it. Mourning produces within a believer God-like qualities that are priceless. The people who are so critical and quick to judge the fallen ones are usually the first ones to seek mercy from God and others when they fall. In the church, we've often treated fallen soldiers without mercy, and discarded them as trash or as unworthy of God's grace. We should all be very willing to extend grace and mercy to others as we would want others to extend them to us in our time of need.

For Godly grief and the pain God is permitted to direct, produce a repentance that leads and contributes to salvation and deliverance from evil, and it never brings regret; but worldly grief (the hopeless sorrow that is characteristic of the pagan world) is deadly (breeding and ending in death). For (you can look back now and) observe what this same godly sorrow has done for you and has produced in you: What eagerness and earnest care to explain and clear yourselves [of all complicity in the condoning of incest], what indignation [at the sin], what alarm, what yearning, what zeal [to do justice to all concerned]. What readiness to mete out punishment [to the offender]! At every point you have proved yourselves cleared and guiltless in the matter.

2 Corinthians 7:10-11 AMP

Mourners become more like Christ when they mourn for the fallen conditions of the hearts of men, and especially for the lost. These mourners understand the misery of sin, not only its consequences on human life, but more importantly on how it breaks the heart of God.

BEATITUDE THREE

Blessed are the meek: for they shall inherit the earth.

Matthew 5:5 KJV

It's much easier to misunderstand the word, "meekness." Many people equate meekness with weakness. They think if you're meek, you'll allow everyone to walk over you. They think it means being timid or passive. What does it really mean to be meek? The Greek word for the word, "meekness" was used to refer to trained animals. For instance, it would refer to a wild, strong and powerful horse that has been trained or tamed so it can be controlled by a human. Meekness, by definition, is great power under control or strength under control. The word, "meekness" used in Matthew 5:5 refers to a God controlled person; a man or woman who has been dealt with by God in a most profound and powerful way so that his entire being comes completely and exclusively under the control of God. A person who is meek has been trained and tamed by God and effortlessly allows himself to submit to all the will of God.

The Scriptures give many examples of people who were meek, and yet strong all at the same time. Moses, the man of God, and who was well known as a great leader, and as having great power with God was described in the Bible for being the meekest man on the face of the earth. He stood up to the most powerful leader in the world and led God's people through the wilderness to the border of the promise land. "Now the man Moses was very meek, above all the men which were upon the face of the earth" — Numbers 12:3. Think about Jesus who could heal the sick and perform astonishing miracles. He spoke to the wind and to the waves and even brought the dead back to life. He said, "Take my yoke upon you, and learn of me; for I am meek and lowly in heart: and ye shall find rest unto your souls" — Matthew 11:29.

WHEN GOD PICKS UP A SHEPHERD BOY AND MAKES HIM A KING

> **Now therefore thus shalt thou say unto my servant David, Thus saith the LORD of hosts, I took thee from the sheepcote, even from following the sheep, that thou shouldest be ruler over my people Israel: And I have been with thee whithersoever thou hast walked, and have cut off all thine enemies from before thee, and have made thee a name like the name of the great men that are in the earth.**
>
> **I Chr. 17:7-8 KJV**

Look at how God picked up David, a shepherd boy, who lived in total obscurity and catapulted him into the limelight as king over Israel. The Lord gave him both success and victory over his enemies and also gave him a great name among the kings of the earth. David's success and notoriety came a result of God's divine favor.

> **Who then is Paul, and who is Apollos, but ministers by whom ye believed, even as the Lord gave to every man I have planted, Apollos watered; but God gave the increase So then neither is he that planteth any thing, neither he that watereth; but God that giveth the increase.**
>
> **I Corinthians 3:5-7 KJV**

The meek recognize God as the source behind their success. The difference between the meek and the humble is that the meek have already attained some type of notoriety. They have influence, success and power, but they're internally detached from all of that success because they know that it all came from God.

> **But by the grace of God I am what I am: and his grace which was bestowed upon me was not in vain; but I labored more**

abundantly than they all: yet not I, but the grace of God which was with me.
I Corinthians 15:10 KJV

People who are meek do not have pride, and are not self-conceited nor do they have an inflated ego or an attachment to self-importance. They do not see themselves more highly than they ought, nor do they walk around with a superiority complex. They are humble, teachable, gentle, modest, submissive, able to be corrected, and full of mercy and compassion.

THE CHARACTERISTICS OF MEEKNESS

1). THE MEEK ARE SPIRITUAL, BUT SOBER MINDED

Brethren, if a man be overtaken in a fault, ye which are spiritual, restore such an one in the spirit of meekness; considering thyself, lest thou also be tempted."
Galatians 6:1 KJV

The meek possess strong values, integrity and moral fortitude. They live by a clear set of convictions and principles and have cultivated strong disciplines over the years. They live cautiously because they understand that no one is immune from potential shortcomings.

2). THEY ARE FULL OF MERCY AND PRAY FOR THOSE WHO FALSELY ACCUSE

And Miriam and Aaron spake against Moses because of the Ethiopian woman whom he had married: for he had married an Ethiopian woman. And they said, Hath the LORD indeed spoken only by Moses? hath he not spoken also by us? And the LORD heard it. (Now the man Moses was very meek, above all the men which were upon the face of the earth. And the LORD spake suddenly unto Moses, and unto Aaron, and unto Miriam, Come out ye three unto the tabernacle of the congregation. And they three came out. And the LORD came down in the pillar of the cloud, and stood in the door of the tabernacle, and called Aaron and Miriam: and they both came forth. And he said, Hear now my words: If there be a prophet among you, I the LORD will make myself known unto him in a vision, and will speak unto him in a dream. My servant Moses is not so, who is faithful in all mine house. With him will I speak mouth to mouth, even apparently, and not in dark speeches; and the similitude of the

LORD shall he behold: wherefore then were ye not afraid to speak against my servant Moses? And the anger of the LORD was kindled against them; and he departed. And the cloud departed from off the tabernacle; and, behold, Miriam became leprous, white as snow: and Aaron looked upon Miriam, and, behold, she was leprous. And Aaron said unto Moses, Alas, my lord, I beseech thee, lay not the sin upon us, wherein we have done foolishly, and wherein we have sinned. Let her not be as one dead, of whom the flesh is half consumed when he cometh out of his mother's womb. And Moses cried unto the LORD, saying, Heal her now, O God, I beseech thee. And the LORD said unto Moses, If her father had but spit in her face, should she not be ashamed seven days? let her be shut out from the camp seven days, and after that let her be received in again. And Miriam was shut out from the camp seven days: and the people journeyed not till Miriam was brought in again.

Num 12:1-15 KJV

Moses interceded for those who falsely accused him and prayed for God's mercy in lieu of judgment. This characteristic is also seen in the life of Stephen the martyr (Acts 7:54-60), and in the life of Christ as depicted on the cross (Luke 23:34).

3). THEY ARE TEACHABLE AND SUBMISSIVE TO GOD

The meek will he guide in judgment: and the meek will he teach his way
Psalm 25:9 KJV

People who are meek are teachable. They understand that one can only understand in part and prophesy in part; hence, no knowledge is conclusive in its infinite state. They know that the minimum requirement for success is continuous education. As a result, they long to grow in a transformative way. Their hearts are pliable, and they are willing to submit to the Word of God (James 1:21).

4). THEY ARE CONTENT IN CHRIST ALONE

The meek shall eat and be satisfied.
Psalm 22:26 KJV

People who are meek know that satisfaction and delight are temporary outside of their relationship with

God. Their identity and contentment are rooted in what is eternal.

5). THEY POSSESS AN UNSHAKABLE CONFIDENCE IN GOD

But the meek shall inherit the earth; and shall delight themselves in the abundance of peace.

Psalm 37:11 KJV

The meek are deeply rooted and grounded in God which enables them to possess a "quiet spirit" (I Peter 3:4). It is a gentle and peaceful spirit that stays calm and in control even in the midst of tests or trials. They just don't have peace; they have abundant peace.

" ... their strength is to sit still"
— Isaiah 30:7 KJV.

" ... in quietness and in confidence shall be your strength"
— Isaiah 30:15 KJV.

6). THEY ARE LOWLY IN HEART

The meek have a deep, inner gratitude towards God and a strong appreciation for life. They understand that life on earth is a gift of trust and use it to live whole-heartedly for God.

Take my yoke upon you, and learn of me; for I am meek and lowly in heart: and ye shall find rest unto your souls.
Matthew 11:29 KJV

7). THEY HAVE A STRONGER PRIVATE LIFE

The meek understand that there is power with God in the secret place. In-fact, the secret place of prayer is the secret to their power. There's so much more to them than meets the eye. I'll say that they pay huge prices in the spirit and make major deposits in the spirit. In this secret place, they settle cases ever before they begin. This is possible because they are firmly rooted in God's Word, which is the backbone of their confidence. The meek are highly skilled swordsmen and swordswomen in the kingdom. The prayer closet is their secret chamber of power where they wield victory after victory in the spirit. And all this confidence comes from the engraftment Word mightily at work in their inner man.

And receive with meekness the engrafted word, which is able to save your souls.
James 1:21 KJV

BEATITUDE FOUR

Blessed are they which do hunger and thirst after righteousness: for they shall be filled.
Matthew 5:6 KJV

Spiritually prosperous are those hungering and thirsting for righteousness, because they themselves shall be filled so as to be completely satisfied.
Matthew 5:6 Went

The Greek word for hunger is "peiná," and it means to be famished or starved. The Greek word for thirst is "dipsao," meaning dryness or to be ardently desirous of something. As water and food is to the body, so is righteousness to the spiritual life. Righteousness is God's way of doing things. When a Christian hungers and thirsts for righteousness they hunger and thirst for His ways. Think about when your physical body becomes both thirsty and hungry, the hunger and thirst cause you to take action. You physically go and get something to drink and eat, don't you? In our spirit, the same thing happens. When we are spiritually hungry, it compels us to go after what satisfies our spirit. We go after God and his word to get spiritually satisfied. Righteousness is very satisfying.

As for me, I will behold thy face in righteousness: I shall be satisfied
Psalm 17:15 NIV

The hunger and thirst to want to see the righteousness of God envelop the earth causes us to take action. We long to see the ways of God dominate the land. We long to fill the earth with the glory of God. It takes a hunger in-born by God's Spirit.

The result of this "hungering and thirsting" is the desire to see righteousness in all aspects of life and society. In order to see the reign and rule of God in the earth, believers need God's passion burning in their hearts, enabling them to declare war against all injustice, lawlessness, wickedness and all works of darkness.

Of the increase of his government and peace there shall be no end, upon the throne of David, and upon his kingdom, to order it, and to establish it with judgment and with justice from henceforth even for ever. The zeal of the LORD of hosts will perform this.
Isaiah 9:7 KJV

BEATITUDE FIVE

> **Blessed are the merciful: for they shall obtain mercy.**
>
> **Matthew 5:7 KJV**

> **Spiritually prosperous are those who are merciful, because they themselves shall be the objects of mercy**
>
> **Matthew 5:7 WENT**

Mercy is such an amazing feature of God's character. The Israelites would often sing that the Lord is good, and His mercy endures forever. God shows mercy to a thousand generations — Deuteronomy 7:9. All of us have benefited tremendously from God's mercy. The truth is without God's mercy, we would have all been consumed.

> **It is of the Lord's mercies that we are not consumed, because his compassions fail not. They are new every morning: great is thy faithfulness.**
>
> **Lamentations 3:22-23 KJV**

Mercy originates from God. And that feature of God's character is transferred to us the moment we give our lives over to Him. We receive mercy from God and are able to transfer it to others. When a person receives a revelation of the gravity of what God has done on his or her behalf through the Lord Jesus Christ, the more natural it would become to extend God's mercy to others. We should always extend mercy to others because God has also showed us undeserving mercy. His compassion, love and forgiveness has been given to us many times over through all our frailties and shortcomings.

> **Be ye merciful, as your Father also is merciful.**
>
> **Luke 35:36**

Showing mercy reminds us all that we're all infallible, and also human. It reminds us that we're righteous only through the righteousness of the Lord Jesus Christ. Righteousness is never earned; it's a gift from God — Romans 5:17. All we did was simply put our faith in the one who accomplished the work of righteousness for us all. We were simply recipients and beneficiaries of His grace. As citizens of the kingdom of God, it is our responsibility to fill the earth with this beatitude of the kingdom. We are to fill the seven spheres of society with heaven's mercy. Imagine, taking God's mercy to the nations of the world in a very practical and tangible way. Imagine us, the church, having such a reserve of wealth and resources enabling us to leverage opportunities to showcase the love of God. Imagine, if we were known for that — the first to shine the light of God in the darkness places of the earth.

BEATITUDE SIX

Blessed are the pure in heart: for they shall see God.

Matthew 5:8 KJV

The heart is the lens through which our view of God is shaped. We cannot see God any better than the state or condition of our hearts. And the heart here speaks of both spirit and soul — Hebrews 4:12. It is important for us that in order to see God more clearly, we must keep our hearts free from all pollutants and contaminants. We must keep it free from anything that would distort our vision of God. If our shades damper, then our vision would be distorted. In the same way, if our hearts contain impurities, our vision would be unclear. To see God as He really is, we must keep our hearts pure. This is important because we would need to continue to reveal to the world the true picture of Jesus, and not a distorted view of Him. If my theology is wrong, my life would be wrong. In other words, it is impossible to live right when one's theology is wrong. Our responsibility as God's people is to fill the earth with the rightness of the kingdom. Our duty is to reveal Him as He really is.

**Beloved, now we are children of God;
and it has not yet been revealed what
we shall be, but we know that when He
is revealed, we shall be like Him, for we
shall see Him as He is. And everyone
who has this hope in Him purifies
himself, just as He is pure.**

I John 3:2-3 KJV

BEATITUDE SEVEN

**Blessed are the peacemakers: for they
shall be called the children of God**

Matthew 5:9 KJV

Peacemakers are people who bring peace. They naturally long for, work for and sacrifice for peace at all cost. It is fair to say that most people love peace, but there is a difference between loving peace and making peace.

**Ye have heard that it hath been said,
Thou shalt love thy neighbor, and hate
thine enemy. But I say unto you, Love
your enemies, bless them that curse
you, do good to them that hate you, and
pray for them which despitefully use
you, and persecute you; That ye may be
the children of your Father which is in
heaven: for he maketh his sun to rise on**

**the evil and on the good, and sendeth
rain on the just and on the unjust**
                                 Matthew 5:43-45

In the above verses, Jesus says that peacemakers are called the sons of God (children of your Father). Peacemakers love their enemies, bless those that curse them and pray for those who persecute them. Peacemaking has to do with destroying the enmity, hostility, bad feelings and tensions between people. God calls believers to love all people, including those with whom they have challenges, differences and offenses. Peacemakers do everything within their power to reconcile mankind back to his maker. They are constantly involved in the ministry of reconciliation, reconnecting people back to God.

**But all things are from God, Who through
Jesus Christ reconciled us to Himself
[received us into favor, brought us into
harmony with Himself] and gave to us
the ministry of reconciliation [that by
word and deed we might aim to bring
others into harmony with Him]. It
was God [personally present] in Christ,
reconciling and restoring the world to
favor with Himself, not counting up and
holding against [men] their trespasses
[but cancelling them], and committing**

to us the message of reconciliation (of the restoration to favor). So we are Christ's ambassadors, God making His appeal as it were through us. We [as Christ's personal representatives] beg you for His sake to lay hold of the divine favor [now offered you] and be reconciled to God. For our sake He made Christ [virtually] to be sin Who knew no sin, so that in and through Him we might become [endued with, viewed as being in, and examples of] the righteousness of God [what we ought to be, approved and acceptable and in right relationship with Him, by His goodness].

2 Corinthians 5:18-21 AMP

The gospel message was given by God to draw humanity back to Him. God is a peacemaking God; He sacrificed his own Son to reconcile the world to Himself and to one another. If God went to such great lengths to bring peace, then believers should also go to great lengths to bring peace. Peacemakers aim for restoration, harmony, and are continually looking for ways, big or small, to create peace.

And how shall they preach, except they be sent? as it is written, How beautiful are the feet of them that preach the

gospel of peace, and bring glad tidings of good things!

Romans 10:15 KJV

BEATITUDE EIGHT

Blessed are they which are persecuted for righteousness' sake: for theirs is the kingdom of heaven.

Matthew 5:10 KJV

You're blessed when your commitment to God provokes persecution. The persecution drives you even deeper into God's kingdom.

Matthew 5:10 MSG

The righteousness spoken of in these Scriptures are two-fold, and they are: the character of rightness and the work of justice.

THE CHARACTER OF RIGHTNESS

Scripture reveals that righteousness is the gift of God's own nature, and is imparted to a believer in the new birth (Romans 5:17), putting him in right standing with God.

This new position of his right standing is without any self-effort. In other words, righteousness is not something one can earn through his own works of goodness. It is a gift meant to be received by faith in Christ Jesus — Ephesians 2:8-9. The "gift" of righteousness was given to empower the believer to reign in life (Romans 5:17), and to live a life well pleasing to God. God's righteousness is never a license to practice sin — Titus 2:11-12. True inward righteousness produces the character of rightness; that is, the desire to live right. Just as the invisible life of the vine is revealed in the fruit it produces, so also is the life of God revealed through the fruit of righteous living.

> **Little children, let no man deceive you: he that doeth righteousness is righteous, even as he is righteous.**
>
> **I John 3:7 KJV**

In a world where so many people live without values and principles, and where there are no rights and wrongs, the church must lead the way in exemplifying the fruits of righteousness. Our lives must become the gospel we preach.

> **In him was life; and the life was the light of men.**
>
> **John 1:4 KJV**

The gospel is the power of God that saves, and that saving power radically transforms us. As light has no concord with darkness, so also must our value systems be so distinct, that it stands apart from the world's value system.

THE WORK OF SOCIAL JUSTICE

When the righteous are in authority, the people rejoice: but when the wicked beareth rule, the people mourn.
Proverbs 29:2 KJV

In a world where systemic injustice and systemic corruption prevails, both in the developing nations and the developed nations of the world, the church must lead the way with social justice and social reformation. These systemic structures, created often by the ruling class, keep a nation, and its people from moving progressively and productively forward. Sadly enough, there are countries all around the world where systemic corruption is not only tolerated, but also encouraged as a means of keeping corrupt leaders in power. Our Lord Jesus openly condemned any hierarchy of power, including the religious hierarchies of His time, who through unjust laws and traditions, sought to keep a people captive and docile. The goal of a righteous government is to create an empowering environment for all of its citizens to succeed and prosper, while serving God wholeheartedly.

Justice and judgment are the habitation of thy throne: mercy and truth shall go before thy face.

Psalms 89:14 KJV

God is a God of justice, equity and righteousness. His throne is established upon it. He cannot, by His own divine nature, tolerate any form of injustice. Scripture has always shown that all forms of injustice ultimately boomerang with God, unless or until repentance and restitution is applied by the faulty party to stay His wrath. God cannot stand the maltreatment of the poor or the weak and neither would He stand for the ill treatment of widows and orphans. Everyone must have a level playing field for winning in life. We must be our brother's keeper. However, most of these systemic issues can only be adequately addressed from the roots. We must look at the root causes, and begin there. We must introduce a paradigm culture to combat the old. It takes about twenty to twenty-five years to fully incorporate into the life of a society a different paradigm of life. Africa had it right when it knew that it took a village to raise a child. Environment is the soil where mindsets, habits and culture are grown. Environment shapes destinies. The end deliverable for the recreation of the earth in Genesis one was to create an environment suitable for man to carry out God's will on earth. And this socio-environmental transformation is a big part of the work of the Great Commission.

The environmental transformation of society primes the people for the triumph of the gospel of our Lord Jesus Christ.

> **And the work of righteousness shall be peace; and the effect of righteousness quietness and assurance for ever. And my people shall dwell in a peaceable habitation, and in sure dwellings, and in quiet resting places.**
>
> **Isaiah 32:17-18 KJV**

The transformation of our environment results in days of heaven upon the earth making it conducive for the work of God's Spirit. It imports the fingerprint of God, stamping it unto every fabric of society. The transformation in itself results into a microcosm of the kingdom of heaven. God's access to people's hearts and minds becomes easier in a "God" predominant atmosphere.

The Great Commission, the commandment to disciple the seven spheres of society, is key to achieving this transformation. We, through the personal transformation of our own hearts and our own minds, and through the personal transformation of our own environments, are able by precept and by practice, to import the same kingdom values into our own respective promise lands. We transmit what we are. God's rule starts from the inside out. Only an egg that breaks from within can give life. God's reign begins as a seed planted in the heart of a man; producing fruits in the mind of the same man, and spreading like a fruitful vine through the life of that same man until it dominates society as a forest. In other words, what God must do through us must be first accomplished in us. That inner work creates the capacity for God to do through us what He intends to accomplish through us. And shouldn't this transformation touch all fields: science, medicine, economics, international relations, politics, education, agriculture, arts and entertainment etc.? I think it should. Believers have been given the power and ability to solve every form of societal ill and injustice in the world, and it is time that we translate our faith into practical and tangible solutions in solving global issues as a means to showing that Jesus is the answer, and the only hope for this world.

THE BEATITUDES AND OUR SALTINESS

All these beatitudes are the salt with which we are to preserve and to flavor our world. Without them, we become saltless; without them, we lose our relevance, and without them we lose our impact. The character of the kingdom of God has a simple and yet, powerful way of exposing the pre-existing Canaanite culture or the darkness of this present evil world. It exposes its vanity and its futility. Although, it was never reported on main news media, the entire Islamic world came under a global crisis centered upon their faith during the ISIS era. That inhumane brutality exercised on Christians exposed irreconcilable issues within the Islamic faith, resulting in millions of souls turning to Christ. Thousands of Imams completely surrendered their lives to Jesus Christ. Many of their influential Imams herald the message of the gospel, and the life of Jesus Christ on public television as the worthy way to treat one's fellow being. That's what the value system of God's kingdom would do, and does do for us wherever it is practiced and lived. These beatitudes are what make Christianity beautiful because they reveal the beauty of our Lord Jesus Christ. The beatitudes are the fragrance that fills a God environment like oxygen fills the air.

Chapter 6:

SEASONING THE WORLD WITH LOVE
"THE NATURE OF THE KING AND HIS KINGDOM"

For God so loved the world that He gave His only begotten Son, that whoever believes in Him should not perish but have everlasting life.

John 3:16 NKJV

Jesus, the Father's embodiment of love came to love people. Our Father God expressed His love through the life of His own son, Jesus. At our worst, He gave us His best, and when we became reconciled with God, He gave us His all. This indeed is the gospel — the gospel of our Lord and Savior, Jesus Christ.

But Christ proved God's passionate love for us by dying in our place while we were still lost and ungodly!

Romans 5:8 TPT

While we were yet sinners, lost eternally and bound for hell, hostile in our hearts toward God, and all that He stands for, and rebellious by nature, God offered us the life of His own son as a ransom for sin. We were not the ones who came searching for God; rather, God came searching for us. He loved us, found us, washed us, filled us and made us His own.

THE SACRIFICIAL LOVE OF CHRIST

Greater love hath no man than this that a man lay down his life for his friends.
John 15:13 KJV

Our Lord Jesus Christ demonstrated His love for us all by offering Himself as the ultimate sacrifice. If the world fully understood, firsthand, the sheer magnitude of His physical and spiritual sufferings, it would at once bow its knees to the Lordship of Christ. Such love is inconceivable and impossible to be grasped by the human mind, and can only be revealed by the Holy Spirit of God. That same love has been shed abroad in our hearts, so that we too, can share it with the world.

For the love of Christ constrained us; because we thus judge, that if one died for all, then were all dead. And that he died for all, that they which live should not henceforth live unto themselves,

but unto him which died for them, and rose again.
                              2 Corinthians 5:14-15 KJV

His love compels us to live for Him. And living for Him is living as He did. It is offering our lives in a way that leads others to Him. I have discovered that there's no greater life than living to bring others to Christ. Life at its fullest happens when all of our thoughts, decisions, actions, assets, and time, are primarily employed in the business of leading the lost to Christ. This alone defines the essence of life.

This is my commandment, that ye love one another, as I have loved you.
                              John 15:12 KJV

A new commandment I give unto you, that ye love one another; as I have loved you, that ye also love one another. By this shall all men know that ye are my disciples, if ye have love one to another.
                              John 13:34-35 KJV

Hereby perceive we the love of God, because he laid down his life for us: and we ought to lay down our lives for the brethren.
                              I John 3:16 KJV

Beloved, if God so loved us, we ought also to love one another. No man hath seen God at any time. If we love one another, God dwelleth in us, and his love is perfected in us.

I John 4:11-12 KJV

God has commanded us to love one another, and only when His love dominates the church would the lost world see Him as He is. Love, God's predominant value system of the kingdom, puts Jesus on display in a way that wins the world to Him. The church, the embodiment of the body of Christ, must live out this trademark of the kingdom in practice as the means of winning the world over. God's love is the most powerful force in the universe. It is inborn by God's Spirit in our born-again spirit — Romans 5:5. God is love, and we are born of God, and therefore, born of love. God's love fights for souls; God's love lives for souls; God's love seeks to save the lost. His love by design must be displayed. God's love is practical.

And regardless of what else you put on, wear love. It's your basic, all-purpose garment. Never be without it.

Colossians 3:14 MSG

THE CHARACTER OF LOVE

Love suffers long and is kind; love does not envy; love does not parade itself, is not puffed up; does not behave rudely, does not seek its own, is not provoked, thinks no evil; does not rejoice in iniquity, but rejoices in the truth.

1 Corinthians 13:4-6 NKJV

LOVE SUFFERS LONG

The Greek word, "makrothumia," is synonymous with the following words: patience, endurance, constancy, steadfastness, forbearance, perseverance, diligence. It is the discipline of possessing a steadfast faith in spite of overwhelming and trying circumstances.

To them who by patient continuance in well doing seek for glory and honor and immortality, eternal life.

Romans 2:7 KJV

This word, "makrothumia," encompasses a disciplined life of faith, unshaken in the midst of unfavorable or challenging circumstances. It is the ability and fortitude to endure unbearable hardship, and injustice for the sake of Christ. This unwavering stance in the midst of trying times demonstrates our trust in God's faithfulness. It shows that He is the God of the mountain as well as the God of the valley. We often see things from one perspective, but God sees all things from all perspectives. Trusting in His faithfulness, in-spite of the daring circumstances, creates ample room for God to fully carry out His perfect work in us, causing all things to work out for our good.

> **Consider it a sheer gift, friends, when tests and challenges come at you from all sides. You know that under pressure, your faith-life is forced into the open and shows its true colors. So don't try to get out of anything prematurely. Let it do its work so you become mature and well-developed, not deficient in any way.**

Developing your faith stamina designed to endure and enjoy hardship as a good soldier puts you on the winning side of life. It grounds you and keeps you from falling apart by providing for you an opportunity for growth. Here, you find your heart anchored on His unfailing love for you empowering you to go through your trials as a victor rather than a victim.

> **And now I want each of you to extend that same intensity toward a full-bodied hope, and keep at it till the finish. Don't**

drag your feet. Be like those who stay the course with committed faith and then get everything promised to them.
Hebrews 6:11-12 MSG

And so, after he had patiently endured, he obtained the promise.
Hebrews 6:15 KJV

The word, "Makrothumia," also means possessing an attitude of forbearance toward the ill treatment from others, including those closest to a person.

Put on therefore, as the elect of God, holy and beloved, bowels of mercies, kindness, humbleness of mind, meekness, longsuffering; forbearing one another, and forgiving one another, if any man have a quarrel against any: even as Christ forgave you, so also do ye.
Col 3:12 -13 KJV

The Bible warned us that offenses will abound always, but believers are called to walk in love and to extend the mercy of Christ, even as He extended His mercy toward us.

With all lowliness and meekness, with longsuffering, forbearing one another in love.

Ephesians 4:2

LOVE IS KIND

You are always and dearly loved by God! So robe yourself with virtues of God, since you have been divinely chosen to be holy. Be merciful as you endeavor to understand others, and be compassionate, showing kindness toward all. Be gentle and humble, unoffendable in your patience with others. Tolerate the weaknesses of those in the family of faith, forgiving one another in the same way you have been graciously forgiven by Jesus Christ. If you find fault with someone, release this same gift of forgiveness to them. For love is supreme and must flow through each of these virtues. Love becomes the mark of true maturity.

Colossians 3:12-14 TPT

Kindness is a kingdom virtue, and we are to clothe ourselves with it. Kindness is the gospel in work clothes. It is the demonstrative gospel, which involves helping, assisting or aiding someone with a particular necessity. It is the art of being hospitable, generous and considerate of others, and alleviating the pain and suffering of others.

> **For he is kind unto the unthankful and the evil.**
>
> **Luke 6:35 KJV**

THE LAW OF KINDNESS

> **When the ear heard me, then it blessed me; and when the eye saw me, it gave witness to me: Because I delivered the poor that cried, and the fatherless, and him that had none to help him. The blessing of him that was ready to perish came upon me: and I caused the widow's heart to sing for joy. I put on righteousness, and it clothed me: my judgment was as a robe and a diadem. I was eyes to the blind, and feet were I to the lame. I was a father to the poor: and the cause which I knew not I searched out. And I brake the jaws of the wicked, and plucked the spoil out of his teeth. Then I said, I shall die in my nest, and I shall multiply my days as the sand. My root was spread**

out by the waters, and the dew lay all night upon my branch. My glory was fresh in me, and my bow was renewed in my hand. Unto me men gave ear, and waited, and kept silence at my counsel. After my words they spake not again; and my speech dropped upon them. And they waited for me as for the rain; and they opened their mouth wide as for the latter rain. If I laughed on them, they believed it not; and the light of my countenance they cast not down.

Job 29:11 -25 KJV

A gospel that cannot be seen is a veiled gospel — 2 Corinthians 4:4. Jesus, not only preached the gospel, but He also showed the gospel — Luke 8:1 KJV. Through acts of mercy and kindness, we can all make a significant difference in people's lives. The saying holds true that people don't care much about what you know, but about how much you care. We are to feed the hungry, clothe the naked, shelter the homeless, provide for widows and orphans, visit the sick and prisoners, pray and win the lost; and in this lies the heart and soul of the ministry of Jesus Christ. This way, we let the light of the gospel shine.

LOVE IS NOT ENVIOUS

Envy can be defined as a state of ill will toward someone, because of some real or presumed advantage experienced by such a person (Louiw and Nida Greek English Lexicon of the New Testament). Envy produces a strong feeling of resentment as a result of other people's accolades, acquisitions or achievements. Often, people are envious because they think that they better deserve what others have. Still, others are envious because someone else has taken the spotlight they think they deserve. Thayer's Greek Lexicon defines it as to be "absolutely heated or to boil with jealousy." Envy is an antithesis to the nature of God. God's love sincerely desires the best for everyone. It rejoices at the success, promotion and progress of others. It even desires that others become greater than themselves.

> **Be kindly affectioned one to another with brotherly love; in honor preferring one another.**
>
> **Rom 12:10 KJV**

Christians are to celebrate and be pleased with the success of others and never give room to the enemy to sow the seeds of bitterness — James 3:14; Gal 5:26.

> **Let nothing be done through strife or vainglory; but in lowliness of mind**

let each esteem other better than themselves. Look not every man on his own things, but every man also on the things of others.

Philippians 2:3-4 KJV

If a person is truly living for the Lord Jesus, and the cause of His kingdom, then, there would be no room for rivalry or jealousy. It is important to avoid worldly competition and comparisons, which are both childish and carnal — 1 Cor. 3:3. Envy is devilish by nature, because it causes strife, divisions and contentions. When people rejoice and celebrate the progress of others, it makes room for them to progress as well.

LOVE IS NOT BOASTFUL

Love is not boastful or vainglorious; it doesn't brag or parade itself haughtily. There is nothing pushy or forceful about the love of God. It is not full of ambition or high-minded.

Be of the same mind one toward another. Mind not high things, but condescend to men of low estate. Be not wise in your own conceits.

Romans 12: 16 KJV

Being boastful is rooted in pride. It flexes with an air of superiority. It is when someone views himself as better or as more important than others. The Bible warns us not think of ourselves more highly than we ought. Even within the church, it is easy to see pastors or church leaders carry themselves in a way that exposes this prideful attitude. An authentic, Christlike humility should be the attitude for us all to take on. Jesus Christ, our Lord is the greatest of all, and yet, a servant of all.

> **For who separates you from the others [as a faction leader]? [Who makes you superior and sets you apart from another, giving you the preeminence?] What have you that was not given to you? If then you received it [from someone], why do you boast as if you had not received [but had gained it by your own efforts]?**
>
> **1 Corinthians 4:7 AMP**

There would be no need to brag or promote oneself if believers understand that all that we are and are ever going to be, and that all that we have and are ever going to have, came from the generous hands of the Father. Every good and perfect gift comes from Him. It is righteous to boast in the Lord, as David did in the face of

Goliath, but it is never right to exhibit a superior attitude toward others.

> **For I say, through the grace given unto me, to every man that is among you, not to think of himself more highly than he ought to think; but to think soberly, according as God hath dealt to every man the measure of faith. Having then gifts differing according to the grace that is given to us, whether prophecy, let us prophesy according to the proportion of faith.**
>
> **Romans 12:3, 6 KJV**

Choose to think of yourself in light of God's grace and mercy. In all of your endeavors, don't compare your work to another's; rather, focus on pleasing God and succeeding in the eyes of Him to which you'd give an account to. Love seeks to give all glory to God and reflects the spirit of meekness in all things. This type of humility inspires others to see the root of one's success and direct the glory and honor and praise to God.

LOVE IS NOT PRIDEFUL

Love is not inflated with pride. The love of God contains no form of arrogance or smugness. From the beginning of time, Lucifer, God's most powerful and most beautiful angel fell because of pride. His fall from heaven was a direct result of the pride that had been brooding in his heart. Apparently, he wasn't content with his most exalted position. He wanted more. He wanted to become God. It is important not to have an exaggerated view of one's own importance.

> **Nay, much more those members of the body, which seem to be more feeble, are necessary: And those members of the body, which we think to be less honorable, upon these we bestow more abundant honor; and our uncomely parts have more abundant comeliness. For our comely parts have no need: but God hath tempered the body together, having given more abundant honor to that part which lacked: That there should be no schism in the body; but that the members should have the same care one for another. And whether one member suffers, all the members suffer with it; or one member be honored, all the members rejoice with it.**
>
> **I Corinthians 12:22- 26 KJV**

Believers have been mandated to love in this manner, and to treat others, not only as they would want to be treated, but also, as Christ Himself treats others; even to those who least deserve it. God hates a prideful spirit because it usurps God's authority. It seeks to enthrone itself in the place of God. Belshazzar is an example of this, "And thou his son, O Belshazzar, hast not humbled thine heart ... but hast lifted up thyself against the Lord of heaven" — Dan 5: 22 -23 KJV. This king allowed his accomplishments to get to his head. He taught he was a god, and the God of heaven had to judge him for that.

> **But he giveth more grace. Wherefore he saith, God resisteth the proud, but giveth grace unto the humble**
> **— James 4:6 KJV.**

The greater the accomplishment, the humbler we need to become, and the more we need to glorify God.

LOVE IS NOT RUDE

Love does not behave in an ugly, indecent and unseemly manner. It avoids disgracing, mistreating or dishonoring someone with the intent of causing harm. Rude people act in defiance of social and moral norms, which results in disgrace, embarrassment, and shame. Love behaves in a manner that believes the best in people. It is approachable and easy to be entreated. God's love is full of kindness and tenderness and believers must take on and exemplify this same love.

Put on therefore, as the elect of God, holy and beloved, bowels of mercies, kindness, humbleness of mind, meekness, longsuffering.

Colossians 3:12 KJV

LOVE IS NOT SELF SEEKING

For all seek their own, not the things which are Jesus Christ's.

Phil 2:21 KJV.

Christ is the perfect example of one who lived a selfless life — 1 John 4:9-10. He gave of Himself, even to the death of the cross. If a person hasn't lived for Christ, then in all actuality, they haven't really lived — Philippians 1: 21. It is making Him the focus and center of one's life that brings true satisfaction. Life is far more than just making a living; it is living for Christ and for the cause of the kingdom. We are to seek first the kingdom of God, and this means that every single part of our lives, live for Him. It is when all about you becomes all about Him. It includes using all that one has, and all that he is to fulfill His cause on earth. We live to serve the ones that Jesus died for: "Look not every man on his own things, but every man also on things of others" — Phil 2:4 KJV.

Then Peter began to say unto him, Lo, we have left all, and have followed thee. And Jesus answered and said, Verily I say unto you, There is no man that hath left house, or brethren, or sisters, or father, or mother, or wife, or children, or lands, for my sake, and the gospel's, But he shall receive an hundredfold now in this time, houses, and brethren, and sisters, and mothers, and children, and lands, with persecutions; and in the world to come eternal life.

Mark 10:28-30 KJV

LOVE IS NOT EASILY PROVOKED

Love is not fretful, resentful, or touchy. It doesn't get easily upset and it is not contentious. It is neither irritable nor is it moody. If these agitations are found prevalent in someone, then, it may point to something deeper. It is a clear sign that a person's emotions are out of control due to the passivity of the inner-man.

If you fall to pieces in a crisis, there wasn't much to you in the first place.
Proverbs 24:10 MSG

When a believer becomes passive about spiritual things, his body and soul take the ascendancy over his spirit man, and as a consequence, opens himself up to all sorts of attacks from the evil one. Little things can easily escalate and be blown out of proportion. This is why God's word encourages believers to be strong in the Lord — Ephesians 6:10.

> **He that hath no rule over his own spirit**
> **is like a city that is broken down, and**
> **without walls.**
>
> **Pr 25:28 KJV**

Passivity is the loss of exercising the will in the control of one's spirit, soul and body — Corinthians 7:37, howbeit, a Holy Spirit empowered will. When the inner-man is not being exercised through a robust communion, the study of the Word and fasting, it remains passive, weakly and sickly. In order to live from a place of victory, a person's spirit man must be exercised to develop strength. This is how a person becomes strong in spirit. Furthermore, it is imperative that Christians learn to walk after the Spirit (Galatians 5:25), mind the Spirit (Romans 8:5), and put spiritual things first. This should not sound strange; it is the normal function of a healthy spirit. When a person's spirit is healthy, it is evidenced by the full operation of the fruit of the spirit (Galatians 5:22); just like healthy fruit is indicative of a healthy tree. Love has self-control — a heart that is free from anxiety, fear, agitation and from all that contaminates the spirit life.

LOVE THINKS NO EVIL

Love keeps no record of wrongdoing. This is a powerful virtue marked in the character of our Lord Jesus Christ. He keeps no record of people's faults and failures. He doesn't even hold a sinner's sin against him — "Not imputing their trespasses unto them" — II Corinthians 5:19. It's cancerous to keep bitter and unforgiving memories in one's mind. It affects the entire nervous system and poisons billions of cells. It is important to be deliberate about not setting one's mind on evil and keeping no record of wrongdoing.

How would you feel, if God remembered all your faults and chose to keep them active in His memory? What if He chose to never to forgive and forget? And how would you feel, if he constantly reminded you of all your shortcomings?

> **For I will be merciful to their unrighteousness, and their sins and their iniquities will I remember no more.**
> **Hebrews 8:12 KJV**

> **I, even I, am he that blotteth out thy transgressions for mine own sake, and will not remember thy sins.**
> **Isaiah 43:25 KJV**

LOVE REJOICES IN THE TRUTH

> **You are of your father, the devil, and
> it is your will to practice the lusts
> and gratify the desires [which are
> characteristic] of your father. He was a
> murderer from the beginning and does
> not stand in the truth, because there
> is no truth in him. When he speaks a
> falsehood, he speaks what is natural to
> him, for he is a liar [himself] and the
> father of lies and of all that is false.**
>
> **John 8:44 AMP**

Satan is a real enemy and should not be taken lightly. He is a liar, a deceiver, a murderer, and he hates the Lord Jesus Christ and His church with a passion. He is out to destroy all things beautiful, and does so by selling his lies or sometimes, incomplete truth.

> **Now the Spirit speaketh expressly, that
> in the latter times some shall depart
> from the faith, giving heed to seducing
> spirits, and doctrines of devils**
>
> **I Tim 4:1 KJV**

Take the issue of abortion for instance. The only way a nation could murder 50 million innocent babies is by believing a lie. This lie has caused more deaths than WWI and WWII combined. Now is the time for the church body to rise up and stand on the pillar of truth.

LOVE IS THE KING'S CHARACTER

In these last days, the church must clothe herself with the character of the King of the Kingdom (Galatians 3:24), if she is to remain relevant and full of power. Nothing can make the church more beautiful than taking on in practice the love-nature of the King. God's expectation for every believer is to grow into the measure of the stature of the fullness of Christ. This measure of the stature of Christ should become our lifestyle. There is no counterfeit for God's love. The world must see Him as He is, and as the church becomes like Him, they will see Him through His church and be transformed by His presence.

HOW LOVE TRANSFORMED AN UNGODLY ENTERPRISE

A young man from Indonesia had inherited multiple businesses from his late father, and among these were a five-star hotel and a motel. The motel, however, was simply a prostitute joint. It was home to well over two thousand prostitution-related activities a week. The young man, unlike his father, was a committed Christian and wanted to transform that motel into a business built and established on Christian values and

Christian principles. After seeking for God's wisdom, he decided to hire some pastors who would come to the motel on a daily basis, not to preach but only to pray. They set up a prayer altar in the motel and started praying for all the prostitutes and also for a total overhaul of the business. For weeks upon weeks, they prayed for these precious souls. After a while, they strategically planned to meet the needs of both the prostitutes and their clients by offering to pray for their needs. Until this point, the gospel message was not being preached. The prostitutes started coming in for prayer and had their hearts transformed in remarkable ways. They were moved by the love of these pastors, who were also serving as host and hostesses. After doing this for 2 years, all the prostitutes were transformed, and as a result, most of their clients were as well. They knew they could no longer continue in their old practices, and therefore, chose to give it up. They were offered further training in order to gain skills for more credible employment. Not only were their souls saved, but the motel was completely transformed into a business that honored God.

This principle may sound very simple, but it always works. If a person really has a heart to reach out and make a difference in people's lives, follow these guidelines: 1) love the lost, 2) build relationships, 3) meet a need and 4) present the gospel. These simple principles are very basic, but the results are very profound.

Chapter 7:

KINGDOM POWER
"WITNESSES OF HIS RESURRECTION"

But ye shall receive power, after that the Holy Ghost is come upon you: and ye shall be witnesses unto me both in Jerusalem, and in all Judaea, and in Samaria, and unto the uttermost part of the earth.

Acts 1:8 KJV

This passage of Scripture has been misunderstood by most within the evangelical community for the past few centuries, and that misunderstanding has robbed us of its true power. This Scripture speaks of being or becoming a specific type of a witness of Jesus, and not necessarily a witness for Christ in a general sense. It is being a witness unto Him, and not a witness for Him. And here lies the key difference. We would let the Scriptures itself explain it. We shall endeavor to trace its strand throughout the "New Testament" usage of the word to help us embrace its fullest meaning, and better appreciate its New Testament application.

WITNESSES OF JESUS BEFORE WITNESSES FOR HIM

> **But when the Comforter is come, whom I will send unto you from the Father, even the Spirit of truth, which proceedeth from the Father, he shall testify of me: And ye also shall bear witness, because ye have been with me from the beginning.**
>
> **John 15:26-27 KJV**

The Holy Spirit Himself is God's greatest witness. He testifies of Jesus, and doth yet testifies. There can never be or will ever be a greater testifier of Jesus than the person of the Holy Spirit. He alone was there from the beginning, originating, initiating, organizing, synchronizing, harmonizing, orchestrating, overseeing, and implementing all the works of Christ from preconception to His exaltation at the right hand of the Father. There can never be another better first-hand account of all the works of our Lord Jesus Christ than that of the Holy Spirit. He singlehandedly authored the Scriptures from where we all receive our own accounts of Christ. And not only does He bear witness of Christ, He is also the principal agent responsible for bearing witness of our Lord Jesus Christ through us all. It is impossible to truly bear witness of Jesus without Him.

> **Wherefore I give you to understand, that no man speaking by the Spirit of God calleth Jesus accursed: and that no man can say that Jesus is the Lord, but by the Holy Ghost.**
>
> **1 Corinthians 12:3 KJV**

He bears witness of Jesus, and we too are to bear witness of Him. However, the Scriptures add a key qualification for this.

> **And ye also shall bear witness, because ye have been with me from the beginning.**
>
> **John 15:27 KJV**

Witnesses of Christ are those who have been with Him from the beginning. A key problem with today's "witnesses" is that you have many witnessing for a person without a witnessing of the person. There are way too many second, third, and fourth-hand account witnesses, instead of being first-hand account witnesses of Jesus. We've been talking much about a Jesus a few have encountered, and continue to encounter. We minister about Jesus without a ministering to Jesus. We speak of old encounters but not fresh encounters. To witness for Him, we must witness

Him — we must remain witnesses of Him. Moses, the man of God witnessed God on Mount Sinai and became a mighty deliverer, and so did Paul the Apostle on the road to Damascus, and so did all the mighty prophets of God. They had so many fresh encounters with God. No man has truly spoken for God who has not met with God, and no man speaks for God who has not first spoken with God. Have you had a firsthand encounter with God lately? Did you meet Him, converse with Him, stay with Him, breathe Him in, downloaded His plans for the hour, receive a living, burning, now word from Him? Only witnesses of Him can witness for Him.

Wherefore of these men which have companied with us all the time that the Lord Jesus went in and out among us, Beginning from the baptism of John, unto that same day that he was taken up from us, must one be ordained to be a witness with us of his resurrection.

Acts 1:21-22 KJV

The almighty Holy Spirit of God comes upon people to make them witnesses of Jesus. He reveals Jesus to men — a living Christ. He sets men on a collision course with God. The Holy Spirit longs to make men witnesses of Christ's resurrection. He's not making story tellers about Jesus; no, He is making men collide with a resurrected Christ. And it is not a one-time collision, but a constant collision. Did you notice that the apostles of old had only one qualification for Apostleship? And what was it exactly? One must be ordained to be a witness with us of His resurrection — Acts 1:22. What kind of a company must we keep? A company of men and women who have witnessed the resurrected Christ. This is primarily what the Holy Spirit has come to do with us — to make us witnesses of His resurrection. He makes us witnesses of actual events — from the baptism of John; through all His three and a half years of ministry, and up until He ascended on high. Witnesses witness Him firsthand. They must have undergone that journey of actually experiencing His crucifixion, death, burial and resurrection. It is impossible to speak with conviction without this experience. It is one thing to know all about flying an aircraft, but an entirely different thing to actually fly one. Show me a single man or woman or male or female mightily used by God that didn't have a tangible or physical encounter with the living God. I can't find one in all of Scripture or in history.

That which was from the beginning, which we have heard, which we have seen with our eyes, which we have looked upon, and our hands have handled, of the Word of life; (For the life was manifested, and we have seen it, and bear witness, and shew unto

you that eternal life, which was with the Father, and was manifested unto us;) That which we have seen and heard declare we unto you, that ye also may have fellowship with us: and truly our fellowship is with the Father, and with his Son Jesus Christ.

1 John 1:1-3 KJV

The apostles of old speak of the seeing, the hearing and the handling of a living Christ. They speak of actual experiences. Encountering God is a real experience, not a figment of one's imagination. Learning to place ourselves in this God atmosphere or God frequency is key.

WITNESSES OF HIS RESURRECTION THROUGHOUT THE BOOK OF ACTS

Men and brethren, let me freely speak unto you of the patriarch David, that he is both dead and buried, and his sepulchre is with us unto this day. Therefore being a prophet, and knowing that God had sworn with an oath to him, that of the fruit of his loins, according to the flesh, he would raise up Christ to sit on his throne; He seeing this before spake of the resurrection of Christ, that

his soul was not left in hell, neither his flesh did see corruption. This Jesus hath God raised up, whereof we all are witnesses.

Acts 2:29-32 KJV

The message of the gospel that the apostles of Jesus Christ preached was the message of His death and His resurrection. This Jesus hath God raised up, whereof we all are witnesses. They were witnesses of His resurrection. They saw Him crucified, dead, buried and raised from the dead. They actually saw or witnessed it. No one had to tell them; they saw it several times. The revelation and conviction of what they had witnessed transformed their lives and message. Peter, the Apostle declares, " ... but such as I have give I to you. In the name of Jesus Christ of Nazareth rise up and walk" — Acts 3:6. Peter knew what he had. Literally, he knew of what he had possessed. He had a living Christ whom he could administer to anyone in need. When you see or witness truth, all doubts dissipate. David the king of Israel saw the death, burial and resurrection of Jesus over one thousand years before Christ was born. He was so identified with it to experiencing it. In Psalms eighty eight, he literally experiences three days in hades in type form. In Psalms sixteen, he experiences the cross. Some experiences are so exact that Jesus relives it one thousand years later. The Holy Spirit took king David through it all foreshadowing the coming of Christ as the lamb of God slained before the foundation of the world. The Holy Spirit transported him into a future vision of the death and resurrection of Christ, and leads him through a life experience of it a thousand years before it was consummated in Christ. That same Holy Spirit can transport us into the past placing us where Jesus, the Christ, was lacerated, crucified, buried and raised from the dead. He can take us all through an actual encounter in the word of God to experience the life of Jesus from the baptism of John through His exalted position at the right hand of the Father.

> **And when Peter saw it, he answered unto the people, Ye men of Israel, why marvel ye at this? or why look ye so earnestly on us, as though by our own power or holiness we had made this man to walk? The God of Abraham, and of Isaac, and of Jacob, the God of our fathers, hath glorified his Son Jesus; whom ye delivered up, and denied him in the presence of Pilate, when he was determined to let him go. But ye denied the Holy One and the Just, and desired a murderer to be granted unto you; And killed the Prince of life, whom God hath raised from the dead; whereof we are witnesses. And his name through**

faith in his name hath made this man strong, whom ye see and know: yea, the faith which is by him hath given him this perfect soundness in the presence of you all.

Acts 3:12-16 KJV

Again, Peter the Apostle boldly declares that Jesus Christ of Nazareth was raised from the dead, and that they are witnesses of His resurrection. The man born lame in his feet was made whole by a living faith in Christ. This faith, the Lord's own faith, was imparted to him to stand on his own two feet. A dead man couldn't do that. It was a living Christ imparting a living faith to raise a forty-year-old man lamed in his feet from birth to perfect wholeness. Because Jesus Christ is very much alive today, He is able to do now all that He did while He was physically present in the earth. Hallelujah, He is the same yesterday, today and forever!

Then Peter and the other apostles answered and said, We ought to obey God rather than men. The God of our fathers raised up Jesus, whom ye slew and hanged on a tree. Him hath God exalted with his right hand to be a Prince and a Saviour, for to give repentance to Israel, and forgiveness of sins. And we are his witnesses of these things; and

**so is also the Holy Ghost, whom God
hath given to them that obey him.**

Acts 5:29-32 KJV

Yes, we are witnesses, and so is the Holy Spirit. The
Holy Spirit bears witness of Jesus' resurrection through
His disciples to the world. Witnessing His resurrection
through the Scriptures in the power of the Holy Spirit
changes a man's ministry for life. Why don't you ask
Him to take you on a personal journey all through
Jesus' life and ministry from the cross to the throne.
Has the Holy Spirit of God placed you at the foot of the
pole where our Lord's body was completely lacerated?
Did you hear the sound of the whip tearing His flesh
to pieces making Him unrecognizable? Has He shown
you which particular stripe took away what particular
disease? Have you seen that disease forever lifted from
you as He forever bore it upon Himself, so that, you'll
never have to bear it again forever? Have you lived
long enough in these realities until it consumed your
very consciousness? O child of God, live and breathe
in them until mortality is swallowed up by immortality.

**How God anointed Jesus of Nazareth
with the Holy Ghost and with power:
who went about doing good, and healing
all that were oppressed of the devil; for
God was with him. And we are witnesses
of all things which he did both in the**

land of the Jews, and in Jerusalem; whom they slew and hanged on a tree: Him God raised up the third day, and shewed him openly; Not to all the people, but unto witnesses chosen before God, even to us, who did eat and drink with him after he rose from the dead.

Acts 10:38-41 KJV

You don't have to be physically present to witness His resurrection. Paul, the Apostle, arguably, the greatest Apostle that ever lived was not physically present when Jesus rose out of that tomb. However, through a direct encounter with Jesus, the Holy Spirit revealed Jesus to him and in him.

But when God, who had chosen me and set me apart before I was born, and called me through His grace, was pleased to reveal His Son in me so that I might preach Him among the Gentiles [as the good news—the way of salvation], I did not immediately consult with anyone [for guidance regarding God's call and His revelation to me].

Galatians 1:15-16 AMP

Jesus was revealed, unveiled, shown or manifested to Paul and in him without any human involvement or agency. This encounter with God wasn't just a one-time thing. All throughout his life and ministry, the Lord Jesus appeared to him so many different times. Paul the Apostle wrote two-thirds of the entire New Testament, and was used mightily by God in bringing the gospel of God's grace to the Gentile world. He spoke of bearing the marks of Jesus on his body as his way of identifying with the sufferings of Christ.

> **But God raised him from the dead: And he was seen many days of them which came up with him from Galilee to Jerusalem, who are his witnesses unto the people.**
>
> **Acts 13:30-31 KJV**

CPSIA information can be obtained
at www.ICGtesting.com
Printed in the USA
BVHW081518080820
585843BV00004B/21

9 781631 299056